HUD Homes for Sale -
Sales and Marketing Guide for Real Estate Agents

By Frances Flynn Thorsen

HOW TO BUILD A SOLID NICHE
IN THE GOVERNMENT HOMES MARKET

HUD Homes
Contract • Transaction • FHA Financing

HUD Homes for Sale: A Complete Buyer's Guide

Disclaimers ... THE RULES and policies and procedures for HUD Homes are constantly changing. Some of the rules change from state to state. HUD made major revisions to the HUD Homes for Sale program throughout 2010. All of this information is substantially correct to the best of the author's knowledge. We welcome input for future revision and change. You can e-mail the author/publisher with your comments at FrancesThorsen@gmail.com. The text references the role of real estate agents in HUD Homes transactions. Real Estate agents are state licensed real estate practitioners. The term real estate agent should not be confused with the term REALTOR® . REALTOR® is a federally registered collective membership mark which identifies a real estate professional who is a member of the NATIONAL ASSOCIATION OF REALTORS® . At this time REALTORS® comprise about half the number of total licensees throughout the United States. A real estate agent does not have to be a REALTOR® to be eligible to sell HUD Homes.

This book is available at special quantity discounts to use as premiums and sales promotions, or for use in corporate and consumer training programs. For more information contact Frances Flynn Thorsen at **FrancesThorsen@gmail.com** or 317-PUBLISH.

HUD HOMES FOR SALE - A Complete Buyer's Guide
Author: Frances Flynn Thorsen
PO Box 64537, Tucson, AZ 85728
317-PUBLISH (phone)
FrancesThorsen@gmail.com (e-mail)

Copyright 2011 Frances Flynn Thorsen
ISBN-13: 978-1460904886
ISBN-10: 1460904885

Library of Congress Catalog Card Number
All Rights Reserved
No part of this book may be reproduced in any form, by any means, without written permission by the publisher except when used in reviews of, or advertisements for, this publication or in other books by the author.
Publisher: Frances Flynn Thorsen

This book is dedicated to some of my special clients who bought HUD homes over the years and who brought joy to my life. The opportunity to know each of them is a gift.

Robin and Tony Anthony
Louise Bringhurst
Lai Bui
Vu Van Bui
Mark Jancsics
Jon and Dana Huber
Joseph Mercado
Tom Yacone
Nabila and Elia Semaan
Kevin Kern
Melissa Marzella and her mothers, Marijo Marzella and Lori Lewis

Table of Contents

Acknowledgements

Lynn Pietrouchie, my colleague and dear friend for 22 years, embodied the essence of HUD's basic mission and Fair Housing. She managed thousands of HUD rentals in the City of Bethlehem, PA, for more than 20 years. She had a magnificent work ethic, keen persistence and unflappable optimism. Her inspiration is priceless. She continues to inspire me. I miss her very much.

My sons **Jens Holger** and **Andreas Holger** send my soul into flight at the mere thought of them or the sounds of their names. My husband **Thor** (poet, proofreader, and provocateur) and I have given the world a gift of two fine men who make the world a better place with each step that they place and each breath of air they take.

Jeremiah Flynn, my father, taught me how to walk, to talk, to pray, to read and to write. **Irene Flynn**, my mother, taught me lessons of faith and unconditional love and forgiveness. I wish they were here to comment on the cover design, proof the pages, and share their ideas. I think I know what they would say. I can feel their smiling embrace. Those thoughts make me feel like I am 12 years old. We are forever young in our parents' hearts. **Linda** is still 11 years old, **Theresa** is seven and **Jerry** will always be my baby brother, six years old.

About the Author

FRANCES FLYNN THORSEN is a free-lance writer, journalist, and real estate course developer. She got her real estate license and became a REALTOR® ® in 1985. She was an early adopter of real estate technology on the Internet. Thorsen was one of the first real estate bloggers to receive national attention early in 2005, with interviews in *Investors' Business Daily*, BusinessWeek Online, Inman News, *REALTOR® ® Magazine*, and *The Philadelphia Inquirer*. She was founding editor of RealTown.com and worked as Community Manager of Trulia.com.

She appeared on Stefan Swanepoel's 2008 list of 50 Most Influential Women in Real Estate in the U.S.

She is the author of "HUD Homes for Sale: A Complete Buyer's Guide" and "HUD Homes for Sale: Sales and Marketing Guide for Real Estate Agents." She is the co-author of "Real Estate Social Media Policies and Procedures Guide" and the companion "Broker Implementation Guide and Workbook."

Thorsen operates an accredited real estate school for real estate agents and brokers continuing education in Arizona.

She works with members of the Arizona Foreclosure Coalition to help distressed homeowners KEEP their homes.

Forward

REAL ESTATE BUYERS are always looking for bargains. New real estate books are published monthly touting ways to find bargains through foreclosures and flipping. Real estate gurus inundate the television air waves with get rich quick schemes that make the gurus rich but hold little promise for most homebuyers and investors.

Many of those schemes are based on an initial premise of fleecing a homeowner of his equity. Many others are based on simple loan fraud. This book does not offer a get rich quick promise. It offers no encouragement to commit fraud. It is a simple "how to" treatise about navigating the HUD Homes For Sale process from start to finish.

This book was first published in 2006. The fourth quarter of 2010 saw a massive redesign of HUD Homes sales and processes. There were more than 55,000 HUD properties in HUD's inventory at the end of 2010 and that number is rising. HUD wants to sell these assets as quickly as possible. This second edition contains information and resources about those changes. HUD Homes is an $8 billion market that will pay $400 million commissions to HUD Homes brokers. It is a highly specialized arena with new rules and regulations. Savvy buyers will reap the benefits of discounted properties.

This book is designed to help you create a niche in HUD Homes, and to excel and differentiate yourself as a government homes specialist in your market area.

There is a fair amount of financing information contained in this book, especially FHA financing. This knowledge is not exclusive to HUD Homes. Over time you will discover you will have many transactions with buyers whose first call is about HUD Homes. Only a fraction of those buyers actually buy HUD Homes. Most of them will buy a property falling into another category -- resale, REO, or investment property.

Most buyers do not get pre-qualified before they speak with a real estate agent. Some 80% of borrowers meet their lenders following referrals from real estate agents. It is wise to develop and nurture strategic alliances with good lenders. Understanding financing is critical to a successful real estate practice. Understanding FHA financing in all its variations is essential to capture a large share of the HUD Homes market in any area.

You will learn to generate leads from ads, mailings, websites, blogs, and numerous other venues.

A grasp of FHA financing and a network of key strategic partners are key to converting those leads to buyers. Helping buyers find homes that meet their wants and needs as well as their budget is gratifying and profitable.

Real estate agents who become HUD Homes specialists will earn the respect of buyers in their market area and they will have the necessary savvy to apply for the privilege of working as local listing brokers. HUD Homes specialists will earn a reputation for excellence and buyers will seek them out as selling agents. -- *Frances Flynn Thorsen*

Disclaimers

THE RULES and policies and procedures for HUD Homes are constantly changing. Some of the rules change from state to state. HUD made major revisions to the HUD Homes for Sale program throughout 2010. All of this information is substantially correct to the best of the author's ability. We welcome input for future revision and change. You can e-mail the author/publisher with your comments at fran@blogmilla.com.

The text references the role of real estate agents in HUD Homes transactions. Real estate agents are state licensed real estate practitioners. The term real estate agent should not be confused with the term REALTOR®. REALTOR® is a federally registered collective membership mark which identifies a real estate professional who is a Member of the NATIONAL ASSOCIATION OF REALTORS®.

At this time REALTORS® represent about half the number of total licensees throughout the United States.

A real estate agent does not have to be a REALTOR® to be eligible to sell HUD Homes.

Chapter One:

WHAT IS A HUD HOME?

HUD HOMES COMPRISE one of the largest inventories of real estate owned (REO) properties in the United States. They are owned by the United States Dept. of Housing and Urban Development (HUD).

A HUD home is a property that has been lost by a previous owner in foreclosure or a property that an owner has given back to the lender with a deed in lieu of foreclosure. Property owners facing financial difficulty, job loss, and medical bills often are unable to keep up with mortgage payments. HUD homes are properties lost by borrowers who defaulted on FHA mortgages.

A lending institution, such as a mortgage company, bank, or savings and loan association, funds a mortgage loan; the Federal Housing Administration (FHA), a HUD agency, insures the mortgage. The mortgage insurance protects the lender from financial loss in the event the borrower defaults. When an FHA homeowner defaults on an FHA loan and the bank takes the house back in foreclosure, the lender has two choices about the disposition of the property:

1. The lender may decide there is sufficient equity in the house to turn a profit; it may keep the property and sell it as part of its Real Estate Owned (REO) inventory.

2. Or, the lender may "cash in" on its FHA insurance policy and turn the property over to HUD. HUD adds the property to its pool of properties in the HUD Homes REO Program.

There are several other ways HUD takes ownership of properties:

- **Deed in Lieu of Foreclosure**: Properties conveyed to HUD by a mortgagee following a deed-in-lieu of foreclosure of an FHA insured mortgage. In this case, the borrower gives the property to the lender without a foreclosure sale and the lender files a claim for FHA mortgage insurance.

- **Custodial Properties**: Properties secured by a second mortgage or home equity conversion mortgage (HECM). These properties are in default and upon inspection by the Field Services Manager (FSM), determined to be vacant or abandoned.

- **Foreclosed Secondary Held Mortgages (SHMs)**: Properties acquired as the result of the foreclosure of a mortgage serviced by HUD including assigned and purchase money mortgages.

- **Home Equity Conversion Mortgages (HECM)**: Properties acquired as the result of foreclosure of a reverse mortgage insured by FHA.

- **Legal Settlement**: Properties acquired as a result of a lawsuit or for other reasons. Sometimes HUD accommodates another federal agency to dispose of real estate assets not insured by FHA.

- **Repurchases/ Buy Backs**: Properties repurchased by HUD to resolve a post sale claim by the purchaser of a HUD Home.

- **184s**: Properties located on Indian or tribal lands and acquired as a result of foreclosure of a loan guaranteed by HUD's Office of Native American Programs (ONAP) under the Section 184, Loan Guarantee for Indian Housing.

- **312s**: Properties acquired as a result of foreclosure.

Who Can Buy a HUD Home?

Any eligible buyer who is pre-qualified by a lender or who has sufficient cash to cover the transaction costs associated with a sale can buy a HUD Home. HUD employees and relatives of HUD employees are eligible to buy HUD Homes with written approval from the Director of HUD's Office of Single Family Asset Management in order to purchase a HUD-owned single-family property.

Buyers do not have to be first-time homebuyers to buy HUD homes.

Buyers do not have to fall into low-income categories.

HUD homes range in price, but most are affordable for low- and moderate-income borrowers.

One of the primary objectives of the program is to provide home ownership opportunities to owner occupant purchasers. Therefore, owner occupant purchasers have priority over investor buyers in the first 30 days that a property is on the market. Investors may not bid on a HUD property during the first 30-day listing period.

An owner occupant purchaser is defined by HUD as a buyer who will live in the property as a primary residence for at least 12 months. An owner occupant purchaser must sign an Owner Occupant Certification Form included in the bid package. (A bid package is available online. It contains a purchase agreement and all addenda necessary to construct a bid for a prospective buyer.)

HUD Homes buyers fall into four categories:

1. Owner Occupants
- given priority in bidding during certain cycles of listing process
- must occupy the house as primary residence for one year
- cannot participate in HUD sales for two years after purchase

2. Good Neighbor Next Door
- police officers, firefighters, emergency medical technicians, and teachers
- 50% discount on list price
- property located in designated Revitalization Area
- must occupy house as sole residence for three years

3. Investors
- cannot bid until Day 31 in initial sales cycle
- no restriction on quantity

4. Government Agencies and Nonprofit Agencies
- must obtain NAID number to bid. . *[NAID is a Name and Address Identifier. HUD requires real estate brokers register for NAID number before becoming eligible to bid on HUD Homes.]*
- access to "First Look" program. *[HUD Secretary Shaun Donovan announced a new Departmental initiative that gives state and local governments and nonprofit organizations participating in HUD's Neighborhood Stabilization Program (NSP) preference to acquire homes from the Department's inventory of foreclosed properties, commonly known as "HUD Homes." Details of the FHA First Look Sales Method have been published as a Notice in the Federal Register. This program is presently being tested in pilot market areas.]*

- bulk purchases of properties on the market more than 60 days
- "Dollar Home" purchases of properties on the market 180 days

Government Homes Arena Specialists

Government agencies and large quasi government agencies are major players in the REO (Real Estate Owned) area. These agencies include:

- U.S. Dept. of Housing and Urban Development (HUD)
- U.S. Dept. of Veterans Affairs (VA)
- Federal Deposit Insurance Corporation (FDIC)
- Fannie Mae
- Freddie Mac
- U.S. Dept. of Agriculture (USDA)
- Internal Revenue Service (IRS)

Each agency has its own rules, its own contracts, and an internal organization devoted to the disposition of real estate assets. Finding qualified and credentialed real estate professionals in the government homes arena is not as simple as picking up the phone and placing random calls to REALTORS® .

Many REALTORS® tout "distressed property" certifications. These are not evidence of HUD Homes and government homes savvy.

Foreclosed properties and distressed properties is a niche with a very wide prism.

HUD Homes is a niche with a finer prism ... achieve home selling success with:

- *Knowledge* about HUD Homes and the transaction process.
- *Access to the tools* to help you find HUD Homes and place successful bids.
- *Plan of action* moving forward.

The Big REO Picture

Foreclosure listings account for approximately 25% of real estate market inventory nationwide (source: Trulia.com and RealtyTrac.com).

Government owned properties comprise about 25% of the foreclosure listings.

Real estate agents face a myriad of changes and challenges in their efforts to keep up to date on new trends and developments, including:

- short sales
- helping consumers meet home retention goals
- working with banks and servicers
- working with government agencies and nonprofits
- risk management
- online auctions and bidding

RealtyTrac.com is the largest online consumer repository of foreclosure data in the country. Their website features rich data and statistics agents can use to study their market areas. This is great information to share on websites and blogs.

ForeclosureRadar.com is another website with useful information real estate agents can use in many market areas.

Who Sells HUD Homes?

HUD Homes for Sale qualified real estate brokers are registered with HUD. *Buyers must work with agents from a registered brokerage; buyers are NOT able to submit bids on their own behalf.* Brokers are listed on HUD's listing website, **www.HUDHomeStore**. Only real estate agents associated with registered offices are allowed to sell HUD properties. Go to **www.HUDHomeStore.com** for listings and a complete list of registered agencies is available at the listing sites.

Becoming an Approved HUD Brokerage

Registering to sell HUD Homes is a simple process. There is no cost to register and all agents who are licensed under the principal broker are included in a single registration. Multi-office firms must register each office separately. Once a registration package is sent to HUD, allow four to eight weeks for processing.

You will receive a HUD NAID (name and address identifier) number after your application is processed; you will need this number to submit bids for HUD properties online. All offers for HUD properties must be submitted online at www.HUDHomeStore.com.

A brokerage that has an expired certification must resubmit an entire original registration package, and the package must be fully processed before bidding privileges are restored. Offices whose privileges expired will not be able to use a temporary NAID number to submit offers; they must wait until they receive their official NAID numbers.

The HUD registration package includes HUD forms SAMS 1111 and 1111A. It is available for download at www.HUDHomeStore.com.

Registration forms contain language that certifies the broker accepts responsibility that all agents comply with all of HUD's requirements. Check the website for the correct address to send the package, and send it with a tracking receipt for your records. Only original documents will be considered; faxes and e-mail submissions are unacceptable.

Brokers must complete paperwork yearly to maintain their status as HUD certified brokers. The certification process used to be valid for longer time periods and HUD certified brokers or agents who are not up to date with their paperwork might be unable to submit bids until that paperwork is completed.

Check with your broker or check the HUD website to be sure that your brokerage is still eligible to submit bids for HUD Homes.

Administering HUD Transactions at the Brokerage

A broker may consider enforcing a policy that all bids are submitted online through an office administrator or through duly appointed agents who are trained to recognize compliant offers and see red flags attached to transactions.

There is approximately 29% fraud rate attached to these transactions, according to HUD. There are strong indications that there will be a crackdown on fraud in the near future. A brokerage-centered bidding procedure may be a prudent choice for risk management purposes, especially in large offices. An important logistical concern in this matter is handling weekend bids. Many owner/occupant bid deadlines fall on Sunday evenings.

HUD master property keys are available through the Local Listing Broker, the brokerage that has responsibility for submitting the HUD listings to the MLS. Electronic lockboxes are installed at HUD properties in many market areas to ensure increased security and tracking.

In areas where master keys are used, the keys can be copied and distributed to individual agents at a HUD registered brokerage with a word of caution: "Do NOT give this key or a copy of this key to any person who is not a licensed agent registered to sell HUD Homes!" Agents are prohibited from sharing keys with buyers and inspectors. **Licensed agents must accompany all showings and be present at all inspections.**

Just because an agency is registered to sell HUD Homes does not mean that the agency or agent does a good job. When it comes to selling HUD Homes there are three classes of agents:

(1) *Agents who excel at the job.* These agents are easy to spot. They will have lots of stories about HUD Homes they sold. They know right off the tops of their heads exactly what HUD Homes are on the market at any given moment, which properties are under contract, recent sale prices, and other pertinent information.

(2) *Agents who are mediocre at best.* These agents rely on information posted on a REALTOR® operated multiple listing service (MLS) rather than the HUD website. Many of these listings appear to be available for a week or longer when they are already under contract. Sometimes listing agents wait until they receive a formal notice from HUD that the paperwork is in order to change a listing status to under contract. This may postdate actual bid acceptance by a week or more. Checking HUD listings on a local MLS service is the least reliable method of determining what is available. The best way to verify availability of a property is to check the listing at www.HUDHomeStore.com.

(3) *The vast majority of real estate agents are generally clueless about the process altogether or terribly out of date.* Most agents have never submitted a bid for a HUD Home and are totally unfamiliar with the process.

It is very important buyers work with capable agents since paper work is critical in these transactions. In the early days of a "new listing under contract" there may be a grace period for making corrections to contracts that are incomplete or drafted incorrectly. There are times, however, when Asset Managers are faced with numerous cancelled agreements. Sometimes they will issue a "zero-tolerance" policy and refuse to accept or sign contracts that are not 100% correct and complete at time of submission.

By the time an agent is finished reading this book he will be able handle a HUD sale expertly and confidently and he will have the means to navigate the HUD Homes for Sale process with clear direction and a plan.

HUD's Mission – Homeownership and Neighborhood Revitalization

HUD has a mission to expand homeownership opportunities and revitalize neighborhoods. Revitalization Areas are HUD-designated geographic areas authorized by Congress under provisions of the National Housing Act. Revitalization Areas are intended to promote "the revitalization, through expanded homeownership opportunities, of revitalization areas."

The criteria for designating an area as a Revitalization Area relate to:

- Household Income,
- Homeownership rate, and
- The incidence of FHA-insured mortgage foreclosure activity in the area.

HUD-owned single family properties located in a Revitalization Area are eligible for discounted sale through special programs in three programs:

1. **Good Neighbor Next Door Program (GNND)** offers police officers, teachers, emergency medical technicians and firefighters 50% discounts on properties located in designated Revitalization Areas. (This topic is covered in depth in Chapter 7).

2. **Asset Control Area (ACA) Program** is aimed at the disposition to eligible participants of HUD-owned properties and future HUD acquisitions of properties and/or mortgage loans located within HUD designated revitalization areas.

3. **Neighborhood Stabilization Project (NSP)** HUD inaugurated a "First Look" program granting nonprofits and government agencies participating in NSP initiatives a first look at HUD Homes before they are offered to consumers. These agencies are purchasing foreclosed homes in targeted areas, rehabbing those properties, and offering them for sale or rent in special programs. Many NSP programs have financial incentives and down payment assistance for eligible buyers.

Major Changes to HUD Home Sales

Late September, 2010, marked a milestone in the history of the HUD Home REO sales program when the United States Department of Housing and Urban Development (HUD) commenced a transition to new contracts with companies to help the agency sell its real estate assets. HUD selected new contractors to serve as Asset Managers (AM), Field Service Managers (FSM), and Mortgagee Compliance Managers (MCM) under the third generation of its Management and Marketing (M&M) program, known as **M&M III**. The new contracts are intended to reduce risk, increase sale prices and accelerate the pace of reselling HUD's inventory of foreclosed FHA homes.

There are five major changes to the program:

1. There are separate contractors for property management (Field Service Managers) and for marketing and sales (Asset Managers).

2. One website houses all data and information – www.HUDHomeStore.com.

3. New bidder registration process encompasses brokers and agents and consumers.

4. Exclusive owner occupant period changes reflect increased emphasis on owner occupant sales.

5. Listings are entered on a daily basis, instead of once a week. Real estate agents and buyers who learn how to use **www.HUDHomeStore** will have a competitive edge in their marketplace.

HUD M&M III Contract Areas

HUD administers the M&M III Contractors Program for REO sales in four regions:

- *Santa Ana Homeownership Center (HOC)* covers the western United States.
- *Denver HOC* covers the middle region of the country.
- *Philadelphia HOC* covers the northeast region.
- *Atlanta HOC* covers the southeastern part of the nation.

The HOCs are charged with the responsibility for registering brokers, assigning NAIDs, and working with the M&M III contractors in those regions.

HUD REO Team Members

HUD outsources its Real Estate Owned (REO) management duties to *regional Marketing and Management (M&M) Contractors* in four regions who prepare the properties for sale and market the homes according to HUD guidelines.

The M&M III program design awards contracts separately to contractors for property management and for marketing and sales -- *Asset Managers* and *Field Service Managers* and *Mortgagee Compliance Managers*.

HUD contracts Oversight Monitors to review Quality Control (QC) of the agency's complete REO portfolio and provide auditing and oversight of the entire disposition process. They also offer market oversight to ensure brokers and agents market properties according to Fair Housing laws and HUD Homes Advertising Guidelines relative to signage, advertising, and Internet marketing.

Asset Manager

The HUD Asset Manager has the following responsibilities:

- Disseminate information about properties to the Local Listing Broker that will place information about HUD Homes in local multiple listing service databases.
- Display the homes on HUDHomes.com when they are available for inspection and open for bids.
- Take bids on the properties.
- Ensure properties are accurately and competitively valued.
- Minimize holding time.
- Select and award a winning bidder.
- Review original sales contracts for accuracy.
- Sign sales contracts on behalf of HUD.
- Authorize utility activation for inspections and appraisals.
- Review and approve extensions to sales contracts.
- Approve the HUD 1 settlement sheets.
- Handle closing and accounting of funds.
- Collect customer service and satisfaction data.

The M&M III Contractor program eliminates the red tape and complex application process for agents and brokers who want to work for HUD as Local Listing Brokers. Asset Managers have the authority to assign Local Listing Broker contracts in their market areas.

Asset Managers are building teams and they are looking for the following differentiators:

- *Quality* in all work and all aspects of working with HUD Homes.
- *Professionalism* interacting with buyers, selling agents, and all parties involved with the HUD Homes selling process.

- *Communication* with buyers and those involved with your transaction. Express your concerns, suggestions, and ideas with your Asset Manager and others as they become evident and you become increasingly involved in the HUD Home selling process.
- *Motivation* to make the sales and move HUD properties!
- *Teamwork* with the real estate community and the Asset Manager to work to the betterment of the HUD sales process and ensure that the process always operates optimally and successfully. Agents play a critical role in the success of the HUD sales program. Asset Managers want to hear from you.
- *Educational Outreach* to consumers and real estate agents. Educational initiative is a key factor in driving sales of HUD Homes.

Mortgagee Compliance Manager

There is a single contractor responsible for HUD's mortgagee compliance issues nationwide, Michaelson, Connor & Boul (MCB), based in Oklahoma. The Mortgagee Compliance Manager is responsible for pre- and post-property conveyance services to ensure HUD's interests are protected.

These services include:

- Review property inspections to ensure property is in conveyance condition.
- Resolve conveyance exceptions.
- Provide guidance to mortgagees related to conveyance responsibilities. Leverage HUD's software and information systems to execute tasks.
- Ensure marketable title.

Field Service Manager

There are multiple Field Service Manager contracts in each HUD region. Field Service Manager (FSM) provides maintenance and preservation services for HUD properties, including:

- Inspect and secure property.
- Clean the home and remove debris.
- Perform cosmetic enhancements/repairs.
- Hire a pest control company to inspect for insects and rodents and order extermination if necessary.
- Order an FHA appraisal.
- Perform a damage assessment of the property.
- Secure the property and be responsible for overall maintenance including minimum lawn care services.

Local Listing Brokers

Asset Managers hire Local Listing Brokers in market areas where HUD properties are located. These designated brokerages are responsible to provide FULL listing services on HUD owned properties in local areas. Local Listing Brokers have the following responsibilities:

- List HUD Homes on the multiple listing service (MLS).
- Prepare property for showings.
- Prepare routine inspections and reports.
- Distribute keys to the selling brokers. In some areas, Local Listing Brokers use electronic lockboxes that are standard security devices in local MLSs. REALTOR® lockbox restrictions present property access challenge to non-MLS agents and brokers who are registered to sell HUD Homes.

Some Local Listing Brokers install a contractor combination lockbox for access by non-REALTOR® licensees. Non-REALTOR® licensees are encouraged to call Local Listing Brokers for access information prior to showing HUD Homes.

- Provide customer service and information resources on HUD listings and the HUD sales process to consumers and real estate licensees.
- Present contract packages to Asset Managers for submission to HUD.
- Hold open houses at HUD Homes. Selling brokers can conduct open houses with written permission from the Asset Manager.
- Provide wide market exposure of the HUD sales process and properties.

Local listing brokers also work with buyers in states where dual agency is allowed, where real estate licensees can work with both the seller and the buyer.

Local Listing Brokers split the real estate sales commission on a HUD Home 50/50 with the selling brokers (working with buyer). The maximum gross commission is 6% -- 3% for Local Listing Broker and 3% for selling broker. In some areas, gross commission may be less than 6%.

The Asset Manager determines both commission amount and the selection of the Local Listing Broker.

Local Listings Brokers may act as selling brokers in states that permit a real estate brokerage to handle both sides of a real estate transaction. Check with the real estate regulatory agency in your state for more information.

The Closing Agent

Another key player in the HUD Homes for Sale game is the Closing Agent. The Closing Agent is a contractor who has duties similar to title companies and escrow companies. The primary function of the Closing Agent is to protect the best interests both of HUD and the Buyer. A partial list of responsibilities includes:

- Schedule settlements (also known as "closings" in some areas of the country).
- Collect earnest money deposit from selling broker at settlement.
- Review loan documents for accuracy.
- Create a HUD 1 Settlement Sheet showing all charges to buyer and seller.
- Collect and receive the funds necessary to purchase the property.
- Close on the property.
- Disburse funds at settlement (i.e. real estate commission, back rents for water and sewer, delinquent taxes, payoff liens, seller proceeds, etc.).

HUDHomeStore Is Superstore Website

A new HUD Homes superstore site, the cyber centerpiece of HUD's new REO program, was launched September, 2010.

HUDHomeStore.com is a one-stop platform containing everything consumers need to know about the HUD REO sales program:

- HUD property information;
- Property disclosures and addenda;
- Real estate and consumer registration features;

- Interactive maps on home page, special programs pages, and property detail pages;
- Resources and contact information for real estate agents and brokers, consumers, state and local governments, and nonprofit organizations.

Agents and consumers welcome HUDHomeStore.com easy navigation, quick page loading, and rich content. The new website replaces a complicated, decade old click route that left many users confused and frustrated.

The new website features all HUD Homes in the country. Agents and consumers have the same view of properties, and access to a myriad of resources and contact information. HUD's new HUDHomeStore.com website was developed by Yardi of Santa Barbara, CA.

Find A HUD Broker / Register for e-Mail Upates

Brokers eligible to sell HUD Homes are listed on **HUDHomeStore** directory.

Brokers and agents are required to register at this website prior to submitting a bid on a HUD property. They must have a HUD NAID (name and address identifier) prior to showing HUD Homes or placing a bid on a HUD property.

Consumers can filter broker search by brokerage or broker name, city, and zip code.

Many real estate agents and brokers operate under the mistaken impression that they can sell HUD Homes because HUD Homes appear in the local multiple listing services. They must submit a registration package to HUD to become eligible to sell HUD properties. That registration must be updated annually and sent via mail to HUD's regional Homeownership Center (HOC).

Consumers and agents can register for property updates using a registration link that appears at the top right of the page. You can search for properties by address, city, state, and zip code.

Find Property Contact Info at HUDHomeStore.com

Each HUD property is assigned a team of experts, including Asset Manager, Field Service Manager, and Local Listing Broker. In some cases, an M&M Contractor is also referenced. Complete contact information is included for each member of the team on the "Agent Info" tab of the Property Info Page:

- Name
- Address
- Telephone number
- E-mail address
- Fax number

Property Condition Reports

The Field Service Manager (FSM) hires inspectors to complete a *Property Condition Report,* and posts the report to the HUDHomeStore.com website with a link at the property listing detail sheet. The *Property Condition Report* contains information about structural and construction details as well as mechanical systems in the property. The FSM also prepares a *Lead Based Paint Initial Inspection Report.*

All of these reports are available on the "Addendums" tab on the Property Detail page when the property is offered for sale. Download these reports if you are working with a buyer who expresses interest in a property.

TIP: Most of these reports will be removed from HUD's website after a bid is accepted. Download copies of all reports prior to that time if you are working with a buyer interested in the property.

Many bids are accepted and fall through due to buyers' inability to get financing. If your buyer does not get a property the first time around, there may be a second opportunity to bid on the home. Sign up for e-mail alerts about new properties. You may see it come on the market again.

Are you new to the HUD Homes market?

If you are new to the HUD Homes for Sale market, there may be another agent or a manager in the office who can serve as a mentor in this process. There are many questions that an agent new to this market will have; good backup in a real estate office is paramount to a successful transaction.

There is a lot of debate within the industry about the role of agents within the context of a business relationship with buyers and a plethora of constructs that define that relationship.

- ❖ Buyer Agency
- ❖ Designated Agency
- ❖ Dual Agency
- ❖ Transactional Agency

Rules and regulations vary from one state to the next relative to the business relationship with consumers and responsibilities of a real estate licensee.

What type of *agency* relationship do you have with your buyers?

Recent pronouncements from HUD argue that selling real estate brokerages DO NOT represent HUD in real estate transactions involving the sale of HUD Homes. There is some confusion about this in some quarters, however; some Asset Managers claim that the selling agency represents HUD unless they are notified in writing that the agency is representing the buyer. Some Asset Managers ask for agency disclosure forms.

There are no prescribed forms for this notice in the HUD package, and there are no proclamations of agency on HUD's website.

HUD will pay the selling agency a commission up to 3% on the sale of a HUD Home, but the matter of establishing an agency relationship with the real estate company remains a matter that is resolved between the homebuyer and the real estate agent.

More Thoughts about Agency and Representation

A business relationship agreement between a home buyer and a real estate broker in most states creates a buyer agency relationship that gives the agent/agency certain fiduciary responsibilities toward the buyer. Buyer agency relationships come in assorted flavors. Agency laws vary from one state to another; the following types of agency relationships are available in most areas:

• An *exclusive buyer agency* relationship specifies the buyer will not enter into a buyer agency relationship with another agent during the term of the agreement. This type of agreement generally notes the agent will be paid a commission, either as a fee or a commission that will be paid upon settlement of a property; or

• A *non-exclusive buyer agency* relationship lets the buyer work with more than one agent at a time. The agent responsible for helping the buyer achieve a sale is the one who will receive a commission; or

• A *transactional agency* relationship does not offer "representation" in a buyer's best interest per se, but lets the agent prepare certain documents without offering a buyer the benefit of advice and counsel and other consultative services.

A *buyer agency relationship* offers a buyer the benefit of "representation" and a range of services that is not available without a written agreement between the parties. For example, in most states, an agent may be able to offer a list of comparable properties to a buyer, but a full-blown market analysis to help a buyer determine fair market value prior to placing an offer on a property is available only within the framework of an agency relationship.

An exclusive buyer agency relationship between a buyer and a real estate agent denotes a business relationship that commits the buyer to working with that agent. That agent, in turn, promises to act in the best interests of the buyer with whom he has a contract.

There is keen competition for HUD Homes among buyers in the large HUD Homes for Sale arena. A prospective HUD home buyer needs to give himself a competitive edge to be successful in this market. Partnership with a good real estate professional is an important step in the process. A buyer does not want to compete with another purchaser for his agent's help and loyalty.

Tech and Web savvy buyers are increasing in number. Most of these buyers want to establish relationships with real estate agents who possess superior computer skills and Internet communication facility. Buyers often are more knowledgeable about HUD Homes than real estate agents.

One Property, Multiple Bids, ONE Successful Bidder!

There is a lot of competition in the market for HUD Homes. Most HUD homes receive multiple bids; in many cases there are numerous bids for a single property.

If a real estate agent is working with multiple buyers for the same property, how does he handle the following questions?

It is reasonable to think that a buyer will WANT and EXPECT guidance to help him achieve an advantage over other buyers in the market. It is an agent's job to provide counsel to provide a competitive edge to secure a property. Here are some key questions a savvy buyer will ask:

"How much is the property worth?"
"How much should I bid?"
"Do you already have other offers on this property?"
"Are you aware of any other offers on this property?"
"Have you written other offer(s) on this property?"
"Do you expect to be writing other offers on this property?"
"How much does your commission rate vary when you are writing bids for HUD homes?"

My personal approach to the issue of showing properties to multiple buyers evolved over years. Some marketing methods generate a tremendous volume of leads for HUD Homes. It is wise to consider how to handle these leads early in the game.

Initially, I showed HUD properties to multiple buyers; sometimes I showed the same property to as many as 10 separate buyers. I wrote a disclosure statement I gave to buyers at our first meeting:

"I often show HUD properties to multiple buyers. I offer each buyer the same information relative to comparable sales. Make your highest and best offer on the property. I will not disclose the specifics of one buyer's bid to another buyer under any circumstances."

Sometimes I wrote three or four offers from different buyers for the same property.

A real estate agent who is actively working the HUD Homes market will often show the same house to multiple buyers. Sometimes an agent will write three or four offers from different buyers for the same property. This situation presents several dilemmas.

- *Only ONE bid is selected for a property.* Spending the time to show a HUD Home to multiple buyers and writing multiple offers is a serious duplication of effort for a real estate agent. Of course, this line of thinking provokes the following question: "Is this transaction about the AGENT or is it about the BUYER?"

- *The exclusive buyer agency contract by all accounts is a one-way street in terms of exclusivity.* A real estate agent may want to measure the worth of exclusivity in a relationship with the buyer during the meeting when he and the buyer come to terms on the specifics of a business relationship agreement. The language pertaining to "showing and presenting the same property to other buyers" generally appears in small type as part of the contract boilerplate. You may consider establishing a "premium" on an exclusive contract that is a two-way street with the following language in a buyer broker contract:

"If you are interested in a property, I will not show it to other buyers. I will work exclusively with you. If I am already working with another buyer on the sale of a property in which you have an interest, I will release you from our contract and let you work with another agent to secure that property."

You may want to consider this scenario and present options to buyers that give you an opportunity to refer business to other agents you know and trust in the event there is a conflict of interest with multiple showings or offers on a HUD Home.

Negotiating the Commission with the Buyer

A Relationship Agreement between a buyer and a real estate brokerage is NEGOTIABLE. Have a frank discussion about commission and your duties as an agent before signing a contract with a client.

The commission is a highly variable factor with enormous impact on the net income to HUD.

An offer of $100,000 with a 6% commission (50/50 Local Listing Broker and Selling Broker) will return $94,000 to HUD.

Another offer of $100,000 with a 5% commission ($3,000 to Local Listing Broker and $2,000 to Selling Broker) will return $95,000 to HUD.

If these are the only two offers on the table for a property listed at $100,000, the offer with a lower commission will yield the winning bid.

It is important to discuss the commission at an early stage with the buyer. Educate the buyer about the value of your services.

Sometimes HUD transactions are very simple. Cash buyers with minimal financial concerns, and properties in excellent condition can offer refreshing opportunities for low-maintenance transactions. On the other hand, some buyers require complex financing to include repair costs. They may have help from family members who need to see the property so that they can offer their input. Some properties are in extreme disrepair and it will be necessary to get initial contractor estimates without the benefit of utilities.

Consider your time and expertise when you discuss compensation with buyers.

"Are you showing the property on a weekend or during evening hours?"

"How many times are you returning to the property?"

"Are you showing it to family members for their approval?"

"Are you meeting contractors at the property to help them determine the cost of repairs and renovation?"

Listing Codes and Financing Categories

An FHA appraisal is ordered shortly after HUD acquires a property, a series of inspections are performed, and reports are sent to HUD's regional office to determine the disposition of the property. The initial listing price is set at the appraised value. Condition of the property determines eligibility for FHA financing. While standard FHA financing requires that properties be in very good to excellent condition, FHA appraisal standards for property condition are a bit more lax for HUD homes.

There are four financing categories for HUD homes:

1. Insurable (IN)

HUD properties that meet FHA minimum property standards qualify for FHA's plain vanilla financing, the FHA 203(b) loan. There is a fair amount of leeway in terms of assessing property condition. HUD "looks the other way" about minor repair issues in appraisals for HUD Homes; sometimes small repair issues become an issue for "clearing" in open market resale transactions.

In this instance NO additional repairs to the property are required for buyers who purchase these properties with FHA financing. Buyers do not have to pay an appraisal fee for FHA 203(b) loans because the lender is required to accept HUD's appraisal when the appraisal is less than 150 days old. (Extensions are granted often to extend the appraisals to 180 days when applications are submitted in a timely manner.)

2. Insurable with repair escrow (IE)

IE properties are available with standard FHA financing and special accommodation for repairs. HUD's inspectors and/or appraiser have determined that the property will meet "minimum property standard" (MPS) if certain repairs are made.

Those repairs must total less than $5,000 in this program. A list of repairs is published, and an amount to complete those repairs is calculated.

A purchaser who buys a home with designated IE using FHA financing will have a separate escrow account created at settlement so that he can complete those repairs. The buyer will be able to borrow money to pay for the repairs and include the cost for those repairs in his mortgage. (For example: A buyer has a winning bid of $100,000 for a HUD home; cost of repairs is $3,000. Cost to purchase the home will be calculated at $103,000.) He will have 90 days to complete the repairs.

In some areas of the country, the escrow amount includes a 10% contingency reserve that can be applied to unexpected or other repairs. Any funds remaining in the account when the work is completed will be applied to the unpaid principal balance of the loan.

Buyers do not have to pay an appraisal fee for FHA 203(b) loans because the lender is required to accept HUD's appraisal. The repair escrow applies only to FHA 203(b) financing and is not available as part of most conventional loan packages. (Note: Some exceptions may apply. Check with your loan officer for information about escrow requirements on HUD home sales.)

3. Uninsurable (UI)

Properties listed UI generally need more extensive repairs (more than $5,000) after closing than IE properties. UI homes suit cash buyers and buyers who are using conventional financing. Use caution with conventional lenders, however, since many of these lenders are also quite particular about property condition and conventional underwriters are leery of HUD homes that carry the UI designation. It is often difficult to obtain financing on a UI property with less than 20% down payment monies.

4. Uninsurable 203(k) (UK)

These Uninsurable properties are available with FHA 203(k) financing, a special acquisition and rehabilitation loan program
FHA 203(k) financing can be used in most HUD property sales. Properties not eligible for this financing will carry a disclosure to that effect on the HUD listing site. This financing can also be used on the IN and IE properties in cases where the purchaser wants to make improvements to the property that will cost more than $5,000. (Note: Not all FHA lenders offer FHA 203(k) financing. Check with your lender for more information.)

Bid Period Timelines

All HUD properties fall into one of four listing periods, hinging upon type of property, bid open date, and days on market.
Properties are added to the market daily.

EXCLUSIVE

Lottery Properties - These properties are placed on the market for five days for special buyer types, including Good Neighbor Next Door program. (In some market areas, there are minor differentiations to listing timelines. Each property listing contains a notice with a bid deadline. Check the property detail page for deadline associated with the property. Listings are the best source of this information.)

NEW Listings – Owner Occupants Only for 30 Days - An Insured (IN)/Insured with Escrow (IE) property not located in a revitalization area that is listed for the first time will be offered for owner occupants only. This property is offered during a period called the OWNER OCCUPANT PRIORITY PERIOD. The exclusive nature of the bid, restricted to owner occupants, lasts for 30 days. Bidding deadline for a new listing ALWAYS ends at midnight.

There are two variants to the sealed bidding process for owner occupants. Check your local listings to determine which applies in your market area.

1. 10-day sealed bidding. Bids accumulate online for the entire length of this period. They are reviewed one business day later. For the remainder of the exclusive owner / occupant priority period, bids are reviewed daily by the Asset Manager.

2. 15-day sealed bidding and 15 days daily bidding with owner/occupant priority. Bids are reviewed on Day 16. For the remainder of the exclusive, owner / occupant priority period, bids will be reviewed daily.

All bids, including investor bids, will be accepted on Day 31 in both instances.

OPEN Listings – All Bidders DAILY - HUD reviews all offers received from owner/occupant bidders during the priority period. If HUD does not receive an offer meeting internal guidelines the listing opens up for bidding to any qualified buyer, including owner occupants and investors. Bid Deadline is DAILY at midnight.

PRICE REDUCTIONS – Owner Occupants First for 5 Days - Sometimes a property does not sell during the open listing period. After several weeks HUD will reduce the price on this property and publish the re-listed property. The first 5 days following a price reduction the property is available to owner occupants only. From time to time HUD listings experience several consecutive price reductions.

OPEN PRICE REDUCTIONS – All Bidders DAILY - Should the property still not sell during the shortened priority period, it then becomes available for bidding to all qualified buyers again. Deadline for bidding is DAILY at midnight.

RE-LISTINGS – Owner Occupants First for 5 Days - Occasionally a property that was already in contract falls out of contract. In that case HUD will offer the property for sale again and re-post the listing. The price may be the same as before or reduced. A re-listed property is available for owner occupants only during the first 5 days.

Open RE-LISTINGS – All Bidders DAILY - If the property does not sell during the priority period for owner occupants, the listing will open up to all bidders with a daily deadline at midnight.

HUD Takes the High Road about Disclosure

HUD has made bold, consumer-friendly advances by offering a full range of property disclosure reports in connection with the sale of its REO properties -- *Lead Paint Report*, an *Environmental Compliance Report*, and a *Property Condition Report*.

Some 30 states presently have laws exempting banks and financial institutions from seller disclosure laws. As the largest federal clearinghouse of foreclosed properties, HUD could choose to travel an easier route, skip the inspections, and discourage inspections on "as is" properties as most banks do with their Real Estate Owned (REO) properties. We think banks should follow HUD's lead; state regulators should recognize the feasibility of inspections and eliminate favorable treatment for banks with respect to seller disclosure laws.

How Are Bids Calculated?

HUD will pay commission up to 3% for the sale of a HUD Home. The commission amount is deducted from the gross sale price to determine the net proceeds to HUD in calculating a winning bid. (Seller assistance up to 3% is also allowed; this reduces the net amount to HUD in like fashion.)

All of the selling costs to HUD -- commissions, seller concessions, are deducted from the gross bid offer.

NOTE: *Repair escrow does not appear as a debit from a gross offer. Repair escrow amount is added to a buyer's mortgage amount. Writing an offer with a repair escrow does not have an adverse impact on net proceeds to HUD in a bid.*

Example One: Mark McBuyer places an offer on a HUD home. His agent will collect the full 3% commission and he is seeking a 3% seller assist to help him with his closing costs. Proceeds to HUD are calculated as follows:

Example One	
Gross Sale Price:	**$100,000**
3% Listing Agent Commission	(3,000)
3% Selling Agent Commission	(3,000)
3% Seller Assist	($3,000)
Net Proceeds to HUD	**$91,000**

Example Two: Katie O'Hara places an offer on the same HUD home. Her agent has agreed to work for a maximum 3% commission. She has enough funds for her down payment and closing costs and does not need any funds for assistance. Her gross offer for the property is $3,000 less than Mark's, $97,000.

Example Two	
Gross Sale Price	**$97,000**
3% Listing Agent Commission	(2,910)
3% Selling Agent Commission	(2,910)
Net Proceeds to HUD	**$91,180**

Even though Katie's offer for the property is $3,000 LESS than Mark's bid, her offer does not include a seller assist (debit) and the real estate commission amounts are less, reflecting higher net proceeds to HUD. This is the number that *really* counts when HUD bids are reviewed and selected.

The commission the real estate agent receives and how that commission is paid is spelled out in a Business Relationship Agreement between the Buyer and the Buyer Agency. Be clear and upfront with buyers about brokerage policy designing bids for HUD Homes.

One Property, Multiple Bids, ONE Successful Bidder!

Sometimes an agent will write three or four offers from different buyers for the same property. This type of situation presents several dilemmas from the standpoint of the real estate agent: time management issues, legal fiduciary concerns, and general matters of integrity.

❖ *There is only ONE bidder who will be selected for the property.* Spending the time to show the property to multiple buyers and writing multiple offers is a serious duplication of effort. However, choosing a single buyer and eschewing the remaining contestants minimizes the opportunity to work with the highest bidder. Of course, this line of thinking provokes the following question: "Is this transaction about the AGENT or is it about the BUYER?"

❖ *The exclusive buyer agency contract by all accounts is a one-way street in terms of exclusivity.* You may want to measure the worth of exclusivity in your relationship with the buyer during the meeting when you and the buyer come to terms on the specifics of a business relationship agreement.

The language pertaining to "showing and presenting the same property to other buyers" generally appears in small type as part of the contract boilerplate. You may consider placing a "premium" on an exclusive contract that is a two-way street:

"If you are interested in a property, I will not show it to other buyers. I will work exclusively with you. If I am already working with another buyer on the sale of a property in which you have an interest, I will release you from our contract and let you work with another agent to secure that property."

You may want to consider this scenario in advance and present options to the buyer that will give you an opportunity to refer him to an agent whom you know and trust in terms of competence and integrity.

❖ *Real estate is about much more than bricks and mortar;* the human element offers compelling challenges. A young couple made an offer on a HUD house in Bethlehem. The first-time home inventory under $100,000 was scarce and the couple had already placed four full-price and better-than-full-price offers on MLS resale properties. They were outbid each time. The HUD house was the house of their dreams. The agent had an offer in hand and the couple's bid came in slightly lower than the bid prepared a day earlier for another buyer. She knew the second buyer's bid would not be the winning offer, but went through all the paces nonetheless. Did she consider urging them to increase their bid? Of course! However, she gave them instructions to give their HIGHEST and BEST offer, and stifled the urge to "goose up" their offer. The agent's decision kept her in alignment with her integrity.

Chapter Two:
GETTING QUALIFIED

Qualifying Number vs. Comfort Zone Number

Buyers must have their financing ducks in a row before placing an offer on a HUD Home. Selecting a good lender is an integral part of the loan process. A lender will take a careful look at a buyer's financial circumstances and calculate how much mortgage the buyer is qualified to receive. This is important to know and it is an important number to weigh against another number that is even MORE important, the maximum monthly mortgage amount a buyer is comfortable paying each month.

What does the buyer pay in rent or toward another mortgage right now?

Is that a comfortable number?

What is the difference between his Qualifying Number and his Comfort Zone Number?

If the Comfort Zone Number is lower than the Qualifying Number, suggest the buyer ask his lender how that number translates into a mortgage amount and use that number as a cap on a mortgage.

Work with the buyer and establish a strict guideline in terms of sale price caps. Don't even look at properties that exceed that level. Don't even be tempted!

There are two dangers in looking at properties with price tags that exceed your Comfort Zone Number:

1. *A buyer may want to extend your financial reach,* but it is wiser to be careful not to stretch your resources so much that you will be "house poor," devoting too many of your monthly dollars to housing expenses. Don't sacrifice too much in other areas of your life to meet a high monthly mortgage obligation. Many people make this mistake. That is a primary reason there are so many HUD Homes for sale.

2. The more expensive a house is the more it has to offer in terms of location and amenities. Lesser-priced houses may pale by comparison with higher priced properties when a buyer is accustomed to looking at higher priced properties. Offer this advice:

"Be kind to yourself. Keep your sights focused on a price range that you can afford right from the beginning. You will avoid having to 'scale down' a search and 'settling' for less."

Trends to maximize purchasing power leave homeowners with debt loads that add a measure of stress to their lives.

Not all lenders finance HUD homes. Not all FHA lenders finance HUD Homes. The best lender is one who has a proven track record of financing HUD Homes.

Ask point blank: "How many HUD homes have you financed in the last two years?"

If a lender is not up to speed on processing HUD Home loans the buyer may become victim to processing delays that extend the transaction past the 45-day deadline for settling the property, and he may incur additional costs for contract extensions. The contract may be extended for 15 days for a per diem fee; the contract may be cancelled by HUD after that if the paperwork is not completed.

Types of Financing For HUD Homes

- **FHA financing** alternatives and guidelines will be explored in depth in following chapters.

- **Conventional and Conforming loans** that conform to Freddie Mac and Fannie Mae standards are designed to finance properties with less than $5,000 of repairs. Check with the lender to be sure that it is possible to set up a repair escrow if necessary. Even if there are no glaring repair issues at first glance, repairs may become evident during the inspection process.

- **Conventional Nonconforming loans,** also known as "A Paper" are available for homes in good condition as well as for properties needing substantial repair. Ask the lender about qualifying for rehabilitation financing. Out-of-pocket costs for this type of financing tend to be higher than the costs for simpler loans, and lenders will want assurances there will be sufficient equity in the home after the repairs are complete.

- **VA financing** (financing for military veterans insured by the U.S. Veterans Administration) is not a good option unless the HUD Home is in excellent condition and requires NO repairs. VA lenders will not accept the FHA appraisal on a HUD Home. If a VA appraiser sees repair issues he will likely call for repairs to be done before settlement. This is not possible on a HUD Home. Buyers who are prequalified for VA financing should speak with their lenders about FHA/VA financing that is designed for military veterans. There are higher cash-out-of-pocket costs associated with FHA/VA financing than plain vanilla VA financing, but it may be the best alternative for a vet who wants to buy a HUD Home.

ACTIVE MILITARY QUALIFIES FOR LOWER INTEREST RATE

The Servicemembers Civil Relief Act passed in the 1940s helps active military personnel cope with financial requirements while on duty. Qualified service personnel can apply for an interest rate reduction not to exceed 6% during active duty. This applies to both commercial and FHA mortgages. The service member must make a request to get this reduced rate. He may also be required to renew his request at periodic intervals as permitted by the Civil Relief Act.

Pre-Qualification Letter

Prior to placing a bid for a buyer a real estate agent must obtain a Pre-Qualification Letter if the transaction involves mortgage financing, or Proof of Funds certification if financing is not necessary.

There are specific Pre-Qualification letter requirements:

- *Original Pre*-Qualification letters are required and must be submitted with all contract packages.
- Pre-Qualification letters must be *signed in blue ink* and must be written on the lender's letterhead. Be sure that it contains contact information for the lender (i.e. mailing address and telephone and fax numbers).
- Pre-Qualification letters should state that a *credit bureau check has been reviewed*. In cash transactions, agents and brokers must provide a *Proof of Funds* letter to verify that there are funds to close and written verification must be submitted on brokerage letterhead stationery.
- All letters (Pre-Qualification and Proof of Funds) must include the HUD Case Number, Property Address, Buyers(s) Name(s), Loan Amount, and Type of Financing.

Ask the lender for a precise *Good Faith Estimate of Closing Costs (GFE)* when he issues a Pre-Qualification letter. The GFE breaks down closing costs and pre-paid expenses due at settlement.

Closing costs on a GFE are related to lender feeds and title fees. The estimate will likely not include the cost of home inspections. Fees for inspections are generally payable at the time that the inspections are performed. These fees are additional to the charges specified on the Good Faith Estimate.

NOTE: Most Good Faith Estimates assume that the buyer and the seller each pay half of the costs for transfer taxes. At this time the HUD Home buyer is responsible to pay the total transfer tax. This cost may be offset if the mortgage lender allows the seller (HUD) to make a contribution for closing costs. FHA will allow the buyer to receive up to a maximum of 3% of the sale price in seller assistance.

If the buyer needs closing cost assistance from HUD, that request is part of the original purchase offer. A buyer whose bid is accepted without a request for closing cost assistance cannot renegotiate the agreement after the fact.

There are many down payment assistance programs available through government agencies and nonprofits in many states. Federal stimulus funds are applied to these programs and in many cases they offer a great alternative to HUD closing cost assistance that reduces the net proceeds to HUD and limits the chances of the buyer to win a property in HUD's online auction.

Check with your local HUD office and nonprofit housing counseling agencies for information about down payment assistance programs in your area.

The lender may have a seller assist cap that is more or less than this amount. Do not assume that the lender will let you receive a full 3% seller assist. Some conventional underwriting guidelines specifically preclude seller assisted financing.

FHA has strict rules for lenders in terms of allowable charges. FHA does not allow lenders and title companies to charge "junk fees" to buyers. There remains confusion about disclosure. The Federal Reserve has a new set of rules on the table relative to compensation disclosure, and there is some indication the central bank will pass on implementation. and final action to the newly created Consumer Financial Protection Bureau (CFPB). Conventional and subprime lending have different sets of rules in terms of fees disclosure.

The Federal Reserve has authority relative to enforcing "The Truth in Lending Act," and HUD has authority relative to settlement service providers. New rulemaking following the housing crisis sees numerous interpretations and conflicts between the rules designed at the Fed and HUD. Experts believe CFPB will consolidate the rules, clarify matters, and minimize confusion.

Once a buyer establishes a working relationship with a lender, it is wise to gather as much documentation as possible so that the lender can expedite loan processing. For a fully documented loan the lender must gather two years of income tax returns, a month of pay stubs, telephone number for employer, recent bank statements and other asset statements, proof of Social Security number, photo identification, landlord references, mortgage account contact information (if applicable), and whatever else the lender requires to complete the loan package.

RESPA Offers Consumers Protection

Congress enacted the Real Estate Settlement and Procedures Act (RESPA) to protect consumers from "…unnecessary high settlement charges caused by certain abusive practices that have developed in some areas of the country."

Prohibited Fees. It is illegal under RESPA for anyone to pay or receive a fee, kickback or anything of value because they agree to refer settlement service business to a particular person or organization. For example, a mortgage lender may not pay a real estate broker $250 for referring a borrower to the lender. It is also illegal for anyone to accept a fee or part of a fee for services if that person has not actually performed settlement services for the fee. For example, a lender may not add a premium to a third party's fee, such as an appraisal fee, and keep the difference.

Permitted Payments. RESPA does not prevent title companies, mortgage brokers, appraisers, attorneys, settlement/closing agents and others, who actually perform a service in connection with the mortgage loan or the settlement, from being paid for the reasonable value of their work.

Penalties. It is a crime for someone to pay or receive an illegal referral fee. The penalty can be a fine, imprisonment or both. A consumer may be entitled to recover three times the amount of the charge for any settlement service by bringing a private lawsuit. If he is successful, the court may also award him court costs and attorney's fees.

Chapter Three:
FHA FINANCING

FHA FINANCING HAS BEEN A MAINSTAY of mortgage lending for many years. In my own market in the Lehigh Valley (PA) and elsewhere, FHA financing accounted for some 75% of total loan volume.

The demise of many subprime loan products creates increased demand for sustainable mortgage financing. FHA has always been the gold standard of sustainable home lending. New regulations governing the lending industry and increased oversight make lending more safe and sensible.

FHA offered the first low-down-payment loan program in the country, opening the door to home ownership for the working class Americans with limited savings. The Federal Housing Administration was established in 1934 with a mission to raise housing standards and design a home financing system with a federal mortgage insurance program that lessens the risk for lenders. The program made homeownership possible for families who were otherwise excluded from the housing market. FHA continues to serve that mandate today.

In the 1940s FHA programs were designed to help financing military housing and for returning veterans and their families.

In following years, through the 1970s, FHA stepped in to help galvanize production of millions of private apartments for elderly, handicapped, and lower income citizenry.

When high inflation and runaway energy costs threatened the economic viability of private multi-family housing units, FHA stepped in with emergency financing to help property owners keep their heads above water.

The 1980s recession offered special financing challenges to homebuyers when private mortgage insurers left oil-producing states. FHA stepped in and helped stabilize declining home prices and designed programs to help homebuyers obtain mortgage financing.

In 1995 FHA placed increased emphasis on minority and first-time homebuyers and implemented the National Homeownership Strategy to provide increased marketing and outreach to those groups.

Advantages of FHA Financing

The housing crisis has seen the demise of many FHA "wannabe" conventional loans and 100% loan products. Conventional financing is tougher than ever, and down payment requirements are hard for many buyers to meet. There is a resurgence of interest in FHA financing nationwide. FHA financing has advantages over conventional financing:

- The total down payment for an FHA loan is only 3.5% of the sale price in most cases. (Prior to the economic meltdown, down payment for FHA financing was 2.25%) Down payment amount requirements may also change to reflect risk factors in credit score. FHA's guidelines call for at least 10% down payment for FICO credit scores between 500 – 580. Down payment requirements and thresholds vary from lender to lender. Check with local lenders for up-to-date information and compare their FHA underwriting policies.

- Income-to-debt ratios are generally higher with FHA loans. Buyers can qualify with 29% front-end ratios and 40% ratios on the back end, compared with similar conventional products that limit borrowers to 33-36% on the back end. Borrowers have more borrowing power with an FHA loan.

Front End Income-to-Debt Ratio: Monthly Income x 29% = Maximum PITI (principal, interest, taxes, and insurance. For a monthly income of $3,000, that means that $870 is the maximum mortgage payment for qualifying purposes UNLESS THE BACK END RATIO NUMBER IS LOWER.

Back End Income-to-Debt Ratio: Monthly Income x 41% - other debt = Maximum PITI (principal, interest, taxes, and insurance). For a monthly income of $3,000, that means that $1,230 minus other monthly debt is the maximum mortgage payment for qualifying purposes. (This reflects other revolving debt such as charge cards, student loans, car loans, etc.)

- HUD lets the buyer negotiate a 3% seller assist toward closing costs for a HUD Home. In many cases, a borrower needs no more than 3% of the total sale price as total cash – out-of-pocket investment. There are other alliances and programs that will let the seller pick up the whole tab. Some of these plans are under close scrutiny by the U.S. Internal Revenue Service.

- FHA is much more lenient with credit issues than conventional lenders. Even bankruptcy discharges a year old can work with FHA if good credit follows the discharge. FHA underwriters give much credence to letters of explanation about credit recitals. (See Chapter 5 "Confronting the Credit Gremlin.")

HUD Homes with FHA financing offer special incentives to buyers. HUD Homes eligible for FHA 203(b) financing have reduced closing costs because there is NO APPRAISAL fee. Lenders are required to use the appraisal that HUD has on file if the appraisal is less than 150 days old. (If you sell a HUD Home near the end of the 150-day window, you can make a written request to HUD to extend appraisal validity 30 days, to 180 days. That request must be in writing two weeks before the 150-day appraisal expiration date.)

Keep in mind an important fact about FHA financing of HUD Homes for Sale: *FHA will only finance a maximum loan amount that corresponds to HUD's asking price.* If a buyer is inclined to 'bid up" a property and finance that property with FHA financing, he will have to make up the difference between the asking price and the bid amount with additional down payment monies. This can put an FHA buyer at a serious disadvantage in the bidding process. It is advisable under these circumstances to have alternative financing in place to maximize bidding potential, if possible.

For instance: A buyer expects that there will be competing bids for a house at 123 Main Street. HUD's list price is $85,000. The buyer is confident that the real value of the property is closer to $100,000. He bids $90,000. His down payment will increase from 3.5% of $85,000 ($2,975 down payment) to that amount PLUS an additional $5,000 ($7,975 total down payment).

Closing Costs HUD Will Always Pay

HUD will pay the costs associated with establishing marketable title for a HUD Home. In addition, the agency will pay the following costs:

- Prorated taxes

- Special assessments
- Homeowner Association fees, if applicable, for the period prior to deed transfer to buyer
- Condominium fees, if applicable
- Cost to provide condominium documents to buyer
- Settlement or Closing Agent for HUD's closing agent. (Purchaser can select a different closing agent at purchaser's expense.)
- Recording fees

Closing Costs HUD Will Sometimes Pay

HUD will help pay a buyer's closing costs in an amount up to 3% of the sale price. HUD may pay for some/all of these closing costs *upon acceptance of a bid including a request for seller assistance*:

- Appraisal fees
- Second appraisal to determine "after rehab" value of a property when FHA 203(k) financing is used
- Flood certification (HUD will play for flood certification if FHA financing is used and the property is located in a flood plain.)
- Up to 3 discount points to buy down the rate
- Up to 1% loan origination fee for FHA and conventional financing
- Up to 1 1/2% loan origination fee for FHA 203(k) financing
- Recording fees
- Transfer taxes
- Survey if required by lender
- Title insurance for lender and/or borrower

NOTE: The amount of seller contribution HUD pays toward closing costs is reflected in reduced net proceeds to HUD. Seller contribution may adversely affect a bid's competitive strength.

Closing Costs HUD Will Never Pay

HUD will not pay the following closing costs:

- Prepaid escrow monies for homeowner association dues
- Prepaid homeowner's insurance
- Prepaid property taxes
- Prepaid flood insurance

Why Some Lenders Don't Want to Offer FHA Financing

Important Note: Not all mortgage companies and lenders are approved by FHA to make FHA loans. Some lenders simply choose not to seek approval because the profit margin with FHA loans is less than the profit that they can generate with other loan products. Others apply for approval but their applications do not survive the approval process. Some lose their ability to offer FHA financing when unseemly professional conduct results in suspension from the program.

There is one, good simple question for a lender that a buyer can ask before doing anything else: "Are you an approved FHA lender?" If the answer is, "No," the buyer may want to move to the next square on his personal Monopoly board.

The simple fact is that mortgage brokers and lenders make more money from subprime loan products than they do from FHA loans. Many of these loan products will never see another application.

New subprime products are finding their way to the market weekly. Beware of lenders who make the following claims:

Lender Claim: *FHA is too picky about property condition.*

Author's Opinion: *FHA makes reasonable demands about property condition.* The benefit to buyers is that they will not likely have major unexpected repair expenses immediately after buying a house. A buyer who has limited funds at the outset will suffer substantial financial hardship when faced with major roof repairs or mechanical failures shortly after moving into a new home. FHA financing offers some safeguards in this regard.

Actually, many responsible conventional lenders are also particular about property condition, but in many conventional transactions, the lenders' concerns about property condition are not communicated until the eleventh hour, throwing many deals into tailspin.

FHA initiated changes to its appraisal standards in November 2005, and eliminated the Valuation and Condition Sheet (VC Sheet) that had a strict, prescribed standard for acknowledging substandard conditions requiring repairs before settlement. New standards eliminate the need for a VC Sheet, and appraisers are expected to follow a more lenient standard in addressing repair issues.

Appraisals of HUD owned properties tend to be much more lenient regarding minor repair issues. There are NO repairs allowed prior to settlement; some repairs (i.e. broken windows, missing handrails, etc.) are noted on the appraisal and the Property Inspection Report but buyers can make repairs at their own leisure after settlement.

Lender Claim: *FHA wants too much paperwork.*

Author's Opinion: FHA requires no more documentation from borrowers than other conventional lenders at prevailing interest rates. Documentation for an FHA loan is no more cumbersome than a fully documented conventional loan. In fact, borrowers have an opportunity to submit additional documentation to establish alternative lines of credit when they have not established traditional lines of credit with the credit repositories. They also have a chance to submit letters of explanation to the lender to explain credit glitches. FHA financing is designed to work for borrowers who are on the road to financial health following setbacks due to extraordinary medical expenses, job loss, divorce, and lifetime episodes that present financial challenges.

The benefit to borrowers is a lower interest rate and better terms than subprime products (that are appealing to mortgage brokers because of their commission potential).

Build Repair Costs Right in the Mortgage

The location is perfect. The property has a great yard. It's large enough and the price is right, BUT

"This property needs too much work!"
"I can't afford to pay for so many repairs!"
"This is just more work in this house than I can do myself!"

Sound familiar?

These are the familiar refrains of buyers who find homes that offer more than a modicum of challenge from a repair and rehabilitation standpoint. Many HUD Homes show more than average wear and tear.

Often properties show evidence of financial hardship suffered by previous owners, deferred maintenance and neglect that often results in the need to repair walls and ceilings, leaking roofs, and lack of attention to mechanical systems (furnaces, plumbing, and electrical components and appliances).

Pandora's Box or Opportunity?

Some buyers may fancy themselves as "handypersons" but balk at the notion of taking on work that will take a big chunk of their liquid cash after settlement.

Real estate pundits may recommend buying a house in need of repair and using sweat equity for increased return on investment. Many buyers have jobs and families and time constraints that make this prospect less attractive than buying a house that is in move-in condition. Counsel your buyer to weigh the expert advice against what "feels right" and follow the path that that suits him best.

FHA offers buyers the chance to complete repairs after settlement with funds that can be financed right in the mortgage. Conventional lenders offer similar products, but FHA rehab loans are the benchmark for the industry. Most conventional rehab loans have seen the same fate as their subprime cousins. FHA 203(k) remains the gold standard for residential rehab financing.

There are two types of FHA rehabilitation loans for the purchase of single-family to four-unit properties in need of rehabilitation:

- *Streamline(K) Limited Repair Program* and
- *FHA203(k)*.

Easy as 1 –2 –3 Rehab Financing

The *Streamline(K)* rolled out in 2005 to assist homeowners with basic repairs costing up to $35,000. This loan can be applied to HUD Homes needing repairs starting at $5,000 to a ceiling of $35,000. It is designed to be an easy-to-use program for uncomplicated rehabilitation and/or improvements for which plans, consultants, engineers, and architects are not required. (More complex improvements are handled with the FHA 203(k) program that is described in the next section.)

Use of the Streamline(K) program is limited to properties with the following work categories:

- Repair/replacement roofs, gutters and downspouts
- Repair/replacement/upgrade of plumbing and electrical systems
- Repair/replacement of existing flooring
- Minor remodeling, such as kitchens, which does not involve structural repairs
- Exterior and interior painting
- Weatherization: including storm windows and doors, insulation, weather stripping, etc.
- Appliances - when at least $3,000 of basic home repairs are involved.
- Appliances may include freestanding ranges, refrigerators, washers/dryers, dishwashers and microwaves
- Improvements for accessibility for persons with disabilities

When a borrower applies for a Streamline(K) mortgage based on repairs identified in a pre-purchase home inspection, he must offer the FHA appraiser information regarding planned repairs and a copy of the pre-purchase home inspection. He must confirm that the repair is necessary and may be accomplished without the need for a fee consultant, work write-up, plans or exhibits.

Additionally, the appraiser must note any health and safety deficiency that the proposed repair plan does not address.

Repairs must comply with all local codes and ordinances and the borrower and/or contractor must obtain all required permits prior to the commencement of work.

FHA 203(k) Repair Program

FHA 203(k) program is designed to handle more robust rehabilitation needs costing at least $5,000 that may include the following types of work:

- Major rehabilitation or major remodeling, such as the relocation of a load bearing wall
- New construction (including room additions)
- Repair of structural damage
- Repairs requiring detailed drawings or architectural exhibits
- Any environmental mitigations including modifications involving disturbance of painted surfaces in pre-1978 properties or any lead based paint abatement
- Landscaping or similar site amenity improvements
- Any repair or improvement requiring a work schedule longer than six months
- Rehabilitation activities that require more than two payments per specialized contractor.

HUD Homes that qualify for FHA 203(k) financing are noted on each property detail page at HUDHomeStore.com.

NOTE: Not all FHA lenders are approved to offer 203(k) financing. Interest rates may be higher for 203(k) financing than it is for less complicated financing that does not include a repair cost component.

FHA Energy Efficient Mortgages

FHA Energy Efficient Mortgages (EEMs) let homebuyers incorporate the cost of energy-efficient improvements into FHA financing. This product is an excellent example of good, common sense mortgage development at FHA where financing is ABOUT THE BUYER. FHA recognizes that reducing energy costs will leave more money in a homeowner's pocket at the end of the month.

Any FHA 203(b) plain vanilla mortgage can include a provision to cover the cost of energy efficient improvements to a property. The cost of the improvements that may be eligible for financing as part of the mortgage is either 5% of the property's value (not to exceed $8,000) or $4,000, whichever is greater.

FHA Graduated Payment Mortgages

FHA Graduated Payment Mortgages are designed for homebuyers who currently have low to moderate income but expect their income to increase substantially over the next five to 10 years. Principal and interest payments start small and increase each year for the next five to 10 years, depending upon the payment plan selected.

FHA Growing Equity Mortgages

FHA Growing Equity Mortgage (GEM) is specially tailored for first-time homebuyers who want to start with small payments that increase gradually over time. As the mortgage payments increase, the additional payment is applied toward the principal of the loan, reducing the mortgage term. GEMs are also attractive to homeowners who want to reduce the term of their mortgage by applying scheduled increases in their monthly payments to the outstanding principal balance.

FHA LOAN CHECKLIST

- ✓ Address of buyer's place of residence (past two years)
- ✓ Social Security numbers
- ✓ Names and location of employers (past two years)
- ✓ Gross monthly salary at current job(s)
- ✓ Pertinent information for all checking and savings accounts
- ✓ Pertinent information for all open loans
- ✓ Complete information for other real estate owned
- ✓ Approximate value of all personal property
- ✓ Certificate of Eligibility and DD-214 (for veterans only, when they are applying for FHA/VA financing)
- ✓ Two most recent pay stubs
- ✓ W-2 forms for past two years
- ✓ Personal tax returns (past two years), current income statement and business balance sheet for self-employed individuals.

Maximum Loan Amounts – FHA, Fannie Mae, Freddie Mac

There are strict mortgage limits for FHA loans.
- Mortgage limits are assigned to each county.
- Mortgage limits are applied to single-family properties, two-unit properties, three-unit properties, and four-unit properties.

You can visit the following website

https://entp.hud.gov/idapp/html/hicostlook.cfm

to check the mortgage limits in your market area.

CY (Calendar Year) 2010 basic standard mortgage limits for FHA insured loans:

	One-Family	Two-Family	Three-Family	Four-Family
FHA Forward	$271,050	$347,000	$419,425	$521,250
HECM	$625,500			
HOPE for Homeowners	$550,440	$704,682	$851,796	$1,058,574
Fannie/Freddie	$417,000	$533,850	$645,300	$801,950

High cost area limits are subject to a ceiling based on a percent of the Freddie Mac Loan Limits. High Cost Area Ceilings for 2010.

	One-Family	Two-Family	Three-Family	Four-Family
FHA Forward	$625,500	$800,775	$967,950	$1,202,925
HECM	$417,000			
Fannie/Freddie	$625,500	$800,775	$967,950	$1,202,925

Section 214 of the National Housing Act provides that mortgage limits for Alaska, Guam, Hawaii, and the Virgin Islands may be adjusted up to 150 percent of the new ceilings. This results in new 2010 ceilings for these areas.

	One-Family	Two-Family	Three-Family	Four-Family
FHA Forward	$938,250	$1,201,162	$1,451,925	$1,804,387
Fannie/Freddie	$938,250	$1,201,162	$1,451,925	$1,804,387

Calculating FHA Mortgages

The following pages contain examples of FHA financing computations. The HUD purchase contract does not require exact mortgage amounts. Still, it is a good exercise and prudent real estate practice to have a working knowledge of financing to determine mortgage amount and cash needs.

The following pages offer an opportunity to calculate several types of loans:

- "Plain vanilla" FHA financing, known as FHA 203(b)
- FHA 203(b) with repair escrow
- FHA 203(k)
- Good Neighbor Next Door FHA borrowers

Calculating Maximum FHA Mortgage 203(b)

Lai and Jerry are buying a HUD home. Sale price is $120,000. List price was $125,000. Property is listed as IN (FHA-insured) and they are making an application for an *FHA 203(b)* loan.

Base mortgage amount is based on the lesser of the sales price or appraised value multiplied by 96.50% (LTV).

- The minimum down payment is 3.5%.

- *Up Front Mortgage Insurance Premium (UFMIP)* calculation is set at 1% of base mortgage amount.

Closing costs may not be financed or used to help meet the minimum 3.5% down payment.

The total first mortgage, including any financed upfront mortgage insurance premium (UFMIP), may not exceed 100% (LTV) Loan to Value / CLTV (Combined Loan to Value) .

The loan amount may not exceed the statutory limit for the area except by the amount of the UFMIP.

The CLTV is not limited to 100% (of the lesser of the sales price or appraised value) when the FHA first lien is combined with a subordinate lien from a government or government agency that is providing down payment and/or closing cost assistance in the form of secondary financing. The maximum mortgage amount for an FHA 203(b) mortgage is shown below.

(NOTE: The UFMIP must be entirely financed into the mortgage [except for any amount less than $1] or paid entirely in cash and all mortgage amounts must be rounded down to a multiple of $1. Any UFMIP amounts paid in cash are added to the total cash settlement requirements. For the purposes of this example and following examples, we will assume the buyer is financing UFMIP.)

Maximum Mortgage on FHA 203(b) Loan

Sale Price	$120,000
Down Payment	(4,200)
Base Mortgage	115,800
Up Front Mortgage Insurance Premium (UFMIP)	1,158
Maximum Mortgage (Base + UFMIP)	**$116,958**

Calculating Maximum FHA Mortgage 203(b) with Repair Escrow

Jesper and Maria are buying a HUD home. Sale price is $130,000. List price was $135,000. Property is listed as IE (Insurable with Repair Escrow) and they are making an application for an *FHA 203(b)* loan. The property needs roof repair, various plumbing fixes, and a new front door. Repair escrow is set at $3,300.

Base mortgage amount is based on the lesser of the sales price or appraised value multiplied by 96.50% (LTV).

- The minimum down payment is 3.5%.

- *Up Front Mortgage Insurance Premium (UFMIP)* calculation is set at 1% of base mortgage amount.

Closing costs may not be financed or used to help meet the minimum 3.5% down payment.

The total first mortgage, including any financed upfront mortgage insurance premium (UFMIP), may not exceed 100% (LTV) Loan to Value / CLTV (Combined Loan to Value) .

The repair escrow is added to the loan amount,

Jesper and Maria will complete the repairs and submit a request for disbursement of funds. The lender will send an inspector and authorize the escrow company to release the funds.

Maximum Mortgage on FHA 203(b) Loan with Repair Escrow

Sale Price	$130,000
Down Payment	(4,550)
Base Mortgage	125,450
Up Front Mortgage Insurance Premium (UFMIP)	1,255
Repair Escrow	3,300
Maximum Mortgage (Base + UFMIP)	**$130,005**

Calculating Maximum FHA Mortgage 203(k)

Robin and Tony are buying a HUD home. Sale price is $80,000. List price was $83,000. Property needs $20,000 in repairs and they are using FHA 203(k) Streamline financing.

Cost of repairs is added to sale price.

Base loan amount is based on the lesser of the sales price plus repairs multiplied by 96.50% (LTV).

The minimum down payment is 3.5% (Sale Price + Cost of Repairs).

UFMIP is 1% of base mortgage amount.

Some closing costs may be financed with 203(k) mortgages. In this exercise, the course will not include financed closing costs in an example. For precise calculations, speak with an FHA 203(k) mortgage lender. (FHA 203(k) financing greater than $35,000 includes additional costs – a fee paid plan reviewer, inspections, and increased budget for "draws" and release of funds.)

Maximum Mortgage on FHA 203(k) Loan

Sale Price	$80,000
Cost of Repairs	20,000
Sale Price + Cost of Repairs	100,000
Down Payment (3.5%)	(3,500)
Base Mortgage	96,500
Up Front Mortgage Insurance Premium (UFMIP)	965
Maximum Mortgage (Base Mortgage + UFMIP)	**97,465**

Calculating Good Neighbor Next Door Max Mortgage

Sean is a police officer who is buying a HUD home in the Good Neighbor Next Door Program. Sale price is $60,000; property list price was $120,000. Property is listed as IN and Sean is making an application for an FHA loan.

Down payment on this GNND house is $100.

UFMIP is 1% of base mortgage amount.

Maximum Mortgage on FHA 203(b) GNND Loan

Sale Price - AMOUNT OF BID	120,000
Adjusted GNND Sale Price - BID x 50%	60,000
Down Payment	(100)
Base Mortgage	59,900
Up Front Mortgage Insurance Premium (UFMIP)	599
Maximum Mortgage (Base + UFMIP)	**$60,499**

Chapter Four:
FHA Underwriting Guidelines

The Federal Housing Administration has specific guidelines for lenders to qualify and approve borrowers for FHA financing. There are guidelines for Buyer Eligibility and guidelines for Property Eligibility.

Buyer Eligibility

Residency

Citizenship of the United States is not required for eligibility.

Permanent Resident Aliens FHA will insure a mortgage made to a lawful permanent resident alien under the same terms and conditions as a U.S. citizen. The borrower must also have a social security number.

Non-Permanent Resident Aliens HUD will also insure a mortgage to nonpermanent resident alien provided the borrower occupies the property as a principal residence. The borrower must have a social security number and be eligible to work in the United States.

Occupancy Requirements

FHA financing is available for owner occupant purchasers only. Borrowers will execute papers to certify their intention to occupy the property as a principal residence. The mortgage documents will not include a reference to the 12-month residency of the HUD Homes for Sale program; there is a separate affidavit that the purchaser will sign. There is a penalty of perjury for purchasers who represent themselves as owner occupants when they are investor buyers. Serious legal consequences for misrepresentation include large fines and incarceration.

Co-borrowers who will NOT occupy the property may be added to the loan application to strengthen a file in some circumstances. This co-borrower must have a principal residence in the United States and be a close family member of the borrower or demonstrate a "long standing" family relationship with the borrower.

Multiple Loans to One Borrower

Owner occupied financing is limited to one primary residence, with the following exceptions that are out of the borrower's control:

- Relocation
- Increase in family size
- Vacating a jointly owned property
- Non-occupying co-borrower
- The borrower must establish bona-fide occupancy within 60 days of signing the security instrument and remain as primary occupant for 12 months.

Co-Borrower/Co-Signer information

Co-borrowers take title to the property and obligate themselves on the mortgage note, including a co-signer with no ownership interest in the property (does not take title) to execute the loan application and mortgage note and, thus, become liable for repayment of the obligation.

The cosigner's income, assets, liabilities, and credit history are included in the determination of credit worthiness.

Military personnel are considered occupant owners and eligible for maximum financing if a member of the immediate family will occupy the property as a principal residence even if the service person is stationed elsewhere.

Minimum Credit Score

When the borrower's credit score is under 620, HUD guidelines refer to underwriter authority level. Underwriters can consider all aspects of the loan, including compensating factors. HUD/FHA established a minimum FICO credit score requirement of 580 for 3.5 percent down payment financing in 2010. Most lenders, however, have a higher credit threshold, 640 -680 and tighter underwriting standards. FHA requires at least 10 percent down payment for borrowers with credit between 500 – 580. [NOTE: It may not be easy to find a lender who will offer underwriting approval with credit scores in the 500s.]

No Credit? FHA underwriters will consider documented alternative credit sources (utilities, cable TV, auto or medical insurance premiums, child care, school tuition, furniture or appliance store accounts) when traditional credit sources are scarce to none.

Bankruptcy

Chapter 7 Bankruptcy   Chapter 7 bankruptcy (liquidation) does not disqualify a borrower from obtaining an FHA mortgage if at least two years have elapsed since the date of the discharge of the bankruptcy. Additionally, the borrower must have re-established good credit or chosen not to incur new credit obligations. The borrower also must have demonstrated a documented ability to responsibly manage his or her financial affairs. An elapsed period of less than two years, but not less than 12 months, may be acceptable if the borrower can show that the bankruptcy was caused by extenuating circumstances beyond his or her control and has since exhibited a documented ability to manage his or her financial affairs in a responsible manner.

Chapter 13 Bankruptcy   A borrower paying off debts under Chapter 13 of the Bankruptcy Act may also qualify if one year of the payout period has elapsed and the borrower's payment performance has been satisfactory. The borrower must receive court approval to enter into the mortgage transaction.

Foreclosure

A borrower whose previous principal residence or other real property was foreclosed or has given a deed-in-lieu of foreclosure within the previous three years is generally not eligible for a new FHA-insured mortgage. However, if the foreclosure was the result of documented extenuating circumstances beyond the control of the borrower and the borrower has re-established good credit since the foreclosure, the lender may grant an exception to the three-year requirement creating a waiting period before the borrower can purchase another home.

Extenuating circumstances include serious illness or death of a wage earner, but do not include the inability to sell the house because of a job transfer or relocation to another area.

Judgments/Tax Liens/Adverse Credit

Court ordered judgments and tax liens must be paid. Exceptions may be granted if the borrower has made regular and timely payments on the judgments and /or tax liens and the creditor is willing to subordinate.

Pay Off Debt to Qualify

Whether installment or revolving: Debts lasting less than ten months must be counted if the amount of the debt affects the borrower's ability to make the mortgage payment during the months immediately after loan closing.

Revolving Debt A minimum 5% of the unpaid balance or $10.00 whichever is greater, must be used to calculate the monthly obligation if no payment is noted on the credit report.

Note: Obligations not to be considered as a debt (nor subtracted from gross income) include: Federal, state and local taxes; FICA or other retirement contributions such as 401(k)s (including repayment of debt secured by these funds), commuting costs, union dues; open accounts with zero balances; automatic deductions to savings accounts; child care and other voluntary deductions; deferred obligations beyond 12 months (i.e. student loans).

Income Requirements

Acceptable Income. A partial list of acceptable miscellaneous sources of income includes child support, alimony, and maintenance payments.

Note: Income requires a copy of the note to establish amount and length of payment (continuance for three years required to use income for qualifying).

Documentation Requirements

- Verification of employment (VOE) and most recent pay stub.
- If the employer will not give telephone confirmation of employment, or if the W-2 indicates inconsistencies (e.g., FICA payments not reflecting earnings), standard employment documentation must be used.
- As an alternative to obtaining a VOE: The lender may choose to obtain from the borrower original pay stub (s) covering the most recent 30-day period, along with original copies of the previous two years' IRS W-2 forms; The pay stub (s) must show the borrower's name, social security number, and year-to-date earnings; The "original" of the W-2 may be any of the copies of the form not submitted with the borrower's income tax returns.
- The lender must also verify by telephone all current employers.

Self-Employed Documentation

Income from self-employment is considered stable and effective if the borrower has been self-employed for two or more years.

The high incidence of failure during the first few years of a new business requires the following for individuals employed less than two years:

Less than one year - The income from borrowers self-employed less than one year may not be considered as effective income.

Between one and two years - An individual self-employed between one and two years must have at least two years previous successful employment (or a combination of one year of employment and formal education or training) in that or a related occupation to be eligible.

Tax Returns

- Federal income tax returns (both individual returns and business returns) for the past two years, with all applicable schedules, for self-employed borrowers.
- Commissioned individuals must also provide individual federal income tax returns for the past two years.
- Signed and dated individual tax returns, plus all applicable schedules, for the most recent two years.
- Signed copies of federal business income tax returns for the last two years, with all applicable schedules, if the business is a corporation, an S corporation, or a partnership.

Fixed Income

Grossing Up. Non-taxable income may be grossed up by 15%. (Child support cannot be grossed up.)

Rental Income is an acceptable income qualifier, subject to proper documentation. 1040s are required for two years. (Depreciation may be added back to the net income or loss shown on schedule E.) Positive rental income is considered gross income for qualifying purposes; negative rental income must be treated as a recurring liability.

Non-Traditional Income

Projected Income. Typically HUD does not accept projected income as a source of acceptable income qualification. If, however, the following criteria are met, the income may be used (the lender may also verify the history of such employment):

- For those borrowers about to start a new job, if the borrower has a guaranteed, non-revocable contract for the new employment that will begin within 60 days of loan closing, the income is acceptable for qualifying purposes.
- The lender must also verify the borrower will have sufficient income or cash reserves to support the mortgage payments and any other obligations during the interim between loan closing and the start of employment.

Employment in Family Business

Borrowers employed by businesses owned by family members are required to provide additional income documentation.

- These borrowers must provide the normal verification of employment and pay stubs, and evidence that he or she is not an owner of the business.

- This may include copies of the borrower's signed personal tax returns or a signed copy of the corporate tax return showing ownership percentages.

Compensating Factors

Underwriters may use compensating factors to counterbalance deficiencies in credit, high debt-to-income ratios, and other antecedents in the loan process.

Some of those factors include:

- The borrower has successfully demonstrated the ability to pay housing expenses equal to or greater than the proposed monthly housing expense for the new mortgage.
- If the borrower over the past 12-24 months has met housing obligations as well as other debts, there should be little reason to doubt the borrower's ability to continue to do so despite having ratios in excess of those prescribed.
- The borrower makes a large down payment toward the purchase of the property. The borrower has demonstrated a conservative attitude toward the use of credit and has shown an ability to accumulate savings.
- Previous credit history shows that the borrower has the ability to devote a greater portion of income to housing expenses.
- The borrower receives compensation or income not reflected in effective income, but directly affecting the ability to pay the mortgage, including food stamps and similar public benefits.
- There is only a minimal increase in the borrower's housing expense.
- The borrower has substantial cash reserves after closing.
- The borrower has substantial nontaxable income (if no adjustment made previously in the ratio computations).

- The borrower has potential for increased earnings, as indicated by job training or education in the borrower's profession.
- The home is being purchased as the result of relocation of the primary wage earner, and the secondary wage-earner who has an established history of employment, is expected to return to work, and there is reasonable prospect for securing employment in a similar occupation in the new area. The underwriter must address the availability of such possible employment.

Down Payment Requirements

Gifts are acceptable if they are from family members up to and including an amount for the entire down payment and all closing costs. (Equity gift is acceptable.) If a gift is transferred at closing from the donor to the borrower or borrower's agent, the source of the gift funds must still be documented as coming from the donor's account. The funds must be further documented with an original, signed **Gift Letter** stating that there is NO REPAYMENT expected and that the gift donor will NOT place a lien on the property.

Other acceptable sources for gifts include close (family type) friend, employer or labor union, a charitable institution, or a governmental agency or public entity that has an FHA-accepted homeownership assistance program.

Seller Contributions

FHA will permit the seller to contribute up to 3% of the property's sales price toward the buyer's actual closing costs, prepaid expenses, discount points, and other financing concessions.

Seller Contributions

Closing costs normally paid by the borrower are considered contributions if paid by the seller. The 3% limitations may include permanent and temporary interest rate buy downs and other payment supplements, payments of mortgage interest (but not principal), mortgage payment protection insurance, and payment of UFMIP (Up-Front Mortgage Insurance Premium).

Property Eligibility

The property itself must meet certain criteria for FHA financing.

Acceptable Properties

- Single family residence
- Manufactured homes
- Condos: Project must be approved and 51% owner-occupancy in project must be verified prior to loan closing.
- PUD's
- Condo spot approvals are acceptable.
- 2 Units
- HUD homes: Appraisals are required. In the case of the purchase of HUD Homes, the lender must accept the HUD-ordered appraisal. The buyer does not have to pay for an additional appraisal.
- Note: 3-4 Units will be considered on a case-by-case basis. Must meet the following guidelines:

❖ "Motivation to Occupy" letter in borrower's own handwriting to include the following verbiage:

"By signing below, I acknowledge that under the terms and conditions of the Note and Deed of Trust securing the subject property, I am obligated to occupy the subject property for a minimum of one year after closing."

Failure to do so would result in the loan being called due and payable and the likely loss of their equity investment. Original to be notarized with loan documents.

❖ Borrower can not own any other property.

Unacceptable Properties

<u>Note:</u> *Since HUD **Homes** carried FHA financing prior to foreclosure it is unlikely that the properties available in this program would fall into any of the categories below. This information is offered for general informational purposes within the context of FHA Underwriting Guidelines.*

- Cooperative and agricultural property
- Commercial enterprises
- Earth homes
- Time-share projects
- Condo-hotel
- Land Trust
- Loft style condominiums
- Projects with pending litigation
- Multi-dwelling condominium
- Partnerships, limited partnerships or corporation ownership
- Boarding houses

- Hotels and motels
- Tourist houses
- Private clubs
- Sanitariums and fraternity or sorority houses

Inspection Reports

Termite Report - Termite/Report & Clearance is required for all FHA financing. *[HUD Homes for Sale Note: HUD will not necessarily perform termite remediation for transactions involving conventional loans or cash. In states where HUD's M&M Contractor does not perform this service prior to listing the property the buyer must assume this cost.]*

Well - HUD requires health authority approval and connection to public system if feasible.

Septic -Septic certifications are only required if the appraiser suspects a problem with the system, or problems are customary in the area. HUD prefers connection to public system if feasible.

Roof - Remaining life expectancy of roof must be two years minimum, or the appraiser will call for repair or re-roofing. All flat roofs require an inspection (exception, i.e. – if the subject roof is part of a large multifamily building, or condominium).

Mechanical Certifications - Instances in which the appraiser is unable to determine if one or all of the systems are working properly may call for plumbing, electrical, and heating certifications. A home inspector, an FHA compliance inspector, or a professional in a specific field must issue a written certification and be deemed qualified by the FHA underwriter.

Municipal Certifications - Code inspections are required in some cities and towns throughout the country. In most cases involving HUD Homes for Sale the buyer assumes responsibility for ordering and paying for a municipal inspection. This inspection must be completed during the Utility Activation period. Uncorrected violations must be resolved AFTER settlement. HUD does not allow any repairs to be made at the property prior to settlement.

Repair Conditions - FHA appraisals are completed on the Fannie Mae appraisal forms and are intended to offer more leniency and flexibility in terms of minor repairs. Completion of minor repairs used to be required for FHA transactions; now completion of minor repairs is no longer mandated for financing.

Clearing Conditions - All items required by the appraiser or underwriter must be inspected and the clearance documented. A licensed, bonded, state registered engineer, licensed home inspector or appropriately registered/licensed tradesperson, as applicable, must provide documentation that all deficiencies have been acceptably corrected upon the completion of the repairs.

RADON WARNING
It's Not All Up To The Bank;
Be Your Own Health Underwriter

Banks and government do not mandate radon testing, even though **radon is the second leading cause of lung cancer in the United States**, according to the United States Surgeon General, the Environmental Protection Agency (EPA) the American Cancer Society, and scientists worldwide.

What is radon and how does it cause cancer?

"Radon is a radioactive gas released from the normal decay of uranium in rocks and soil. It is an invisible, odorless, tasteless gas that seeps up through the ground...Radon decays quickly, giving off tiny radioactive particles. When inhaled, these radioactive particles can damage the cells that line the lung. Long-term exposure to radon can lead to lung cancer...proven to be associated with inhaling radon," according to NCI.

Some years ago when residential radon came on the health radar screens, federal guidelines were developed that recommended residential remediation at levels that were substantially lower than levels in Canada and Europe. Critics cried "foul" and accused the government of pandering to radon remediation companies who were likely to reap more dollars from more stringent guidelines. Time, however, has proven the critics wrong on all counts. Studies published in *The American Journal of Epidemiology* point to higher incidents of lung cancer occurring even in households where the radon levels are at the low end of that scale.

A British report goes even further with the potential for radon risk: "... calculations suggest that the dose to the basal layers of the skin may also be high, with a consequent possible risk of skin cancer.

Unless countermeasures are taken, a smaller number of people may also run a significant risk of stomach cancer from radon ingested in drinking water." (UK National Radiological Protection Board, published in Journal of Radiological Protection 2002)

We urge you to have your homes tested for radon. We also urge you to stop smoking. The best way to beat lung cancer is to take a preventive approach. Test your home for radon. Keep your family safe and healthy.

Chapter Five:

CONFRONTING THE CREDIT GREMLIN

"I DON'T THINK I'LL EVER BE ABLE TO BUY A HOUSE. My credit is terrible." I wish I had a nickel for every house I sold to buyers who said that to me at an initial meeting or over the phone in the last 25 years. Most of those people were wrong, and they purchased homes with FHA financing.

There are ways to handle EVERY type of credit issue. Sometimes after a review of the circumstances we devise a plan that lets the buyer take some period of time to resolve dispute, pay down some debt, save a little more cash, and establish credit history where there is none.

This chapter will offer some tools and resources to help you and your lender analyze the situation carefully and help devise a plan and a strategy for financial recovery.

Understanding Credit Challenges

Many buyers suffer financial hardship stemming from life events beyond their control. Unemployment, illness, death, and divorce can introduce financial misfortunes that seem overwhelming. Accompanying feelings of desperation and hopelessness compound the problem when a prospective buyer adopts an attitude of resignation to his plight.

Credit reports are mathematical tools that quickly weigh the negative impact of these challenges as a predictor of the person's willingness and ability to pay future debt. Credit reporting agencies are slow to correct mistakes and to measure improvement in quantifiable terms. They do not measure more human prognosticators of creditworthiness. The human factor gets a voice, a chance to explain, an opportunity for financial redemption.

FHA underwriters are trained to weigh human circumstances. A carefully written Letter of Explanation can go a long way toward getting a loan approved. FHA wrote the book about second chances.

CREDIT REPORTING AGENCIES

Trans Union
(800) 888-4213

Equifax
(800) 997-2493

Experian
(888) 397-3742

Letter of Explanation

Obtain a copy of your credit report. You can get a copy of your credit report at *www.AnnualCreditReport.com*. Consumers are entitled to a free copy of their reports from each bureau every 12 months. Write an explanation for each derogatory entry as well as for recent "soft" inquiries. Be sure to include the following components for each entry:

1. Cite the entry or inquiry first with the creditor name, the amount of monies involved, and the date(s).

2. Explain the history of the problem. Don't be timid about sharing the details of personal challenges. Be honest about the circumstances that led to your financial problems. If circumstances were beyond your control, give a brief history of the events leading to your inability to meet your financial obligations. Life impacting personal events and emotions attached to them are important factors an underwriter considers. On the other hand, if you were remiss in your obligations, and the problems were due to your own negligence, be candid and admit your mistake. Follow this admission with a statement that you understand the importance of establishing a good credit profile and emphasize that you now place a priority on paying your bills on time. Remember, this letter is written for HUMAN eyes, not for a computer.

3. Describe the steps you took to correct the problem. "I paid the amount owed," or "I entered into a payment arrangement" are good starters, especially if you can provide documentation for your claims.

4. Close the letter with a paragraph that pulls it all together and describes a pattern of improved financial health habits. Project creditworthy loan performance and give the underwriter an "A" right here for approving your loan application! A sample appears on the following pages.

5. Supply documentation to support your narrative.

- **Divorce matters** can be documented with divorce decree or separation agreement, court ordered documents for child support, tax documents for most recent year filing jointly, paperwork pertaining to arrearages in child support, and printout from domestic relations court showing either satisfactory child payment history or arrearages.
- **Job Loss** claims can be supported with layoff notice, Unemployment Office records, and other proofs of dismissal.
- **Injury Resulting in Inability to Work** can be shown with proof of Workman's Compensation and letters from doctor or employer about the injury.
- **Spousal Abuse** can be documented with police reports, medical records, and Protection from Abuse orders from the court.
- **Business Failure** is best illustrated with tax returns for the most recent year or proof that the borrower is no longer self employed (i.e. current pay stub from employer).

SAMPLE LETTER OF EXPLANATION
FOR CREDIT CHALLENGED BUYERS

Re: FHA Mortgage Application

Dear Sir or Madam:

This letter provides explanations for each item listed in my credit report obtained in connection with my mortgage application.

1. Unpaid Student Loan Collection Balance Due $1,224. Pennsylvania State University. Dated 11/09 and 04/09

These are duplicate items on the credit report. In May 2009, I graduated from Penn State. At this time I moved in with a friend at 123 Hamilton Ave. in State College because I was not able to find a job. I found a job four months later and moved into an apartment at 334 College Avenue.

My loan deferment period expired at that time and I commenced payments on a regular basis. I was under the impression that the loan that I received for prior education at Lock Haven University was included in these payments because I never received a bill from Lock Haven University.

In 2010 I received a note from a former roommate at Lock Haven that contained unopened mail that she kept for me. There were bills from Lock Haven University totaling $3,200. I immediately sent them $1,000 and additional monies in the following months. I will pay this loan in full before closing.

2. Late Payments Dated 10/09, 11/09, and 12/09 and 04/10 with Current Student Loan Balance $14,224

When I moved in September 2009 I inadvertently missed a payment on my student loan. Each of the payments I made in the following months was logged as 30 days late. I caught up as soon as it was brought to my attention

In March 2010 my brother suffered an injury at work and was unable to make his rent and some other obligations. I tried to help him meet some of those expenses, and missed one of my own as a result. I brought my account up to date shortly thereafter and have paid this bill on time each month ever since.

3. Late Payments Dated 01/10, 03/010, 04/010, and 05/10 with Credit Card Bank. Current Balance Zero

In January 2010 there was a charge on my credit card bill that I did not authorize. I did not pay the bill because I did not order the product. That amount was removed from my bill the following month. From a period of March through May 2010, I made large payments to bring my student loan up to date (see above) and I was short of funds as a result. I should have balanced my payments so that nothing else suffered. I know that paying my bills is important for my future and for the future of my family.

4. Late **Payments Dated 02/10 – 05/10 with Universal Bank Group. Current Balance Zero**

I believe that this is a mistake on the credit report. I have never had an account with this bank. I am disputing the entry with the credit reporting agency.

5. **Late Payments with US LEC**

I always contested this bill. US LEC was charging me for services associated with my web services that I did not use. These charges were attached to legitimate charges and when I became aware of the fact that I had already paid for these services for two years I tried to persuade them that it was unfair to charge me for services I did not use. They did not agree and in the end I paid the $325 bill to restore my credit and then I cancelled my account with them.

6. **Why Five Banks Checked My Credit in the Last Three Months**

I spoke with several lenders in the last three months to compare rates and terms to find a mortgage.

I appreciate the opportunity to share information about the circumstances leading to less than satisfactory entries on my credit report. My credit rating is very important to me and I am striving to meet all of my financial obligations in a responsible manner. I am excited about owning my own house and I look forward to building a strong relationship with you as a lender. You will see that I will make all of my payments on time and I promise that you will be happy that you approved this loan.

Yours truly,
Fiona Murphy

Establish New Credit with PRBC

"I don't have bad credit; I just don't have any credit." How does someone establish credit? Conventional wisdom says, "Borrow some money and pay it back."People are putting themselves into debt to establish a credit score that did not recognize the payments that they were already making. Pay Rent, Build Credit, Inc. (PRBC) is a web-based self-help service that enables consumers and small business owners to build their credit scores through timely rent, mortgage, and other recurring bill payments.

"The PRBC Data Network enables users to build an historical credit file using multiple payment accounts such as rent, mortgage, mobile home, utilities, student loan, auto, insurance, phone, self-storage, etc... Users can build an accurate credit file with rent and other bill payments in real time when made online, by phone, credit or debit card, ACH (automated clearing house), or by other means that can send a date-stamped electronic "receipt" to PRBC.

"PRBC users can build historical credit files based on up to three years of prior payment records that can be manually verified by independent sources, like banks, REALTORS®, accountants, and credit counselors. But most importantly, the PRBC Data Network enables consumers and small business owners to build an accurate credit file automatically.

"The results for consumers can be staggering. Without going into debt, a renter can prove they are ready, willing, and able to handle a big financial obligation, like repaying a mortgage. The PRBC Data Network will provide a greater number of loan applicants with an equal opportunity to access prime rate mortgages, auto loans, and other financial products...

"This is a significant development for borrowers and lenders alike because until now, credit reporting and scoring technologies have not been able to account for the timeliness of most rental, sub-prime loan, utilities, and other household or business related bill payments as a measure of credit worthiness.

"The PRBC Data Network will accept...rental and other bill payment input from landlords, mortgage lenders, and other creditors who want to use the PRBC Data Network to report timely, as well as late payments, to reward their customers who pay on time, not just penalizing those who are late."

Chapter Six:

INVESTOR BUYERS

INVESTORS ARE ELIGIBLE to purchase HUD Homes after the property has been on the market for 30 days without an acceptable bid from an owner occupant purchaser. An investor may purchase only one HUD Home every two years.

There are some different rules for investors in the HUD Homes for Sale program.

Investors are welcome to conduct a full battery of inspections, but cancellation of the contract due to a home inspection report may result in forfeiture of the investor's earnest money deposit.

There are many investors who check the owner occupant box with the full knowledge that they will NEVER occupy the property. This constitutes fraud and poses risks of fine and incarceration.

Why HUD Fraud Is Unchecked

Rampant, long-term abuse of the HUD Homes for Sale program remains unenforced and unchecked. A HUD audit report published several years ago pointed to more than 41,000 fraudulent HUD Homes sales transactions.

HUD's own estimates value those transactions at $2.9 billion between 1995 and 2001.

HUD properties are offered for sale during an initial exclusive bidding period to individuals who certify that they will occupy the property for 12 months, and those purchasers have not purchased a HUD property within two years. A HUD homebuyer who buys a property as an owner occupant is required to sign an affidavit containing a caveat that there is a $250,000 fine for misrepresenting his/her intent to occupy the property.

A 1998 HUD memorandum stated "...the purpose of the Single Family Property Disposition Sales Program is to reduce the inventory of acquired properties in a manner that expands homeownership opportunities, strengthens neighborhoods and communities, and ensures a maximum return to the mortgage insurance fund. While both owner-occupant and investor purchasers may purchase HUD-owned properties, HUD's sales procedures are structured to enhance opportunities for owner-occupant purchasers. There have, nonetheless, been cases of alleged abuse where investors may have misrepresented themselves as owner occupants when bidding on HUD-owned properties."

My personal experience with HUD home sales goes back to the early 90s, when new listings in this area (Lehigh Valley, PA) appeared in *The Philadelphia Inquirer* on Wednesday mornings; a single agent in a tiny office in Easton (PA) had the single HUD key for the entire Lehigh Valley inventory of HUD Homes; Agents sent signed contracts via overnight express mail for public bid openings on Monday mornings in Philadelphia. HUD properties were not listed in the MLS at that time; buyers needed substantial deposit monies; and inspections were not allowed.

Owner occupants were virtually locked out of the market due to large down payment cash requirements and serious financing restrictions.

When the Clinton Administration took office, HUD Secretary Henry Cisneros quickly enacted reforms that gave priority to owner occupant purchasers in the bidding process, made properties available for sale with low down-payment FHA financing, and offered buyers a chance to order home inspections. Bid results were announced via telephone message recordings after the public bid openings. Agents and buyers calling to check on bid status would hear the property address, bid sale price, the name of the selling agent, and the PURCHASER'S NAME.

Occasionally, this agent (and others) would hear the name of a prominent local investor trying the pull the wool over HUD's eyes, and strike a real estate bargain at the expense of legitimate bidders. It would take a couple of telephone calls to HUD and the selling agent, a reminder about the ramifications of fraud, and ultimately the bid would be awarded to the next highest bidder with owner occupant status.

Bid results on the Internet contain information about proceeds to HUD and the selling agency, but NO information about the successful bidder. It is impossible to use the present system to monitor fraudulent activity at this juncture. Investors are still perpetrating fraud in large numbers.

HUD's Inspector General and enforcement resources are stretched to the limit with large scale mortgage fraud operations and other issues arising fueling a national housing crisis. There are insufficient human assets in the trenches to catch and prosecute investors posing as owner occupants, stealing homeownership opportunities from legitimate bidders.

Invoking the Freedom of Information Act for additional information prior to publishing the first edition of this book, I was unable to document a single instance of a HUD prosecution involving investors misrepresenting themselves as owner occupants.

I've made a recommendation for reform over and over again in my blogs: Publish the names of the purchasers when bid results are posted. It is a simple matter to add those fields to a Bid Results page. Eagle-eyed real estate agents and buyers nationwide will police the results and expose the investor culprits long before they go to settlement. It is a complex problem with an easy solution.

On the other hand, other types of HUD Single Family Home Sales Fraud are prosecuted mightily:

1. An investor in Grand Rapids, WI, disguised his company as a nonprofit group to acquire more than two dozen homes at about $500 each. Properties were rehabbed and sold. Estimated loss to HUD is about $2 million.

2. Federal officials demanded repayment of about $1.2 million from 54 police officers and teachers who defrauded a program that helped them buy houses in return for living in poor, crime-ridden neighborhoods. Police officers and teachers in Miami (FL), Manassas (VA), Memphis (TN), and Springfield (MA), Dallas (TX), District of Columbia, and New Orleans(LA), rented out, sold or abandoned the homes in violation of their contracts. An Essex County (NJ) Sheriff's Officer pleaded guilty to fraud.

Others were able to secure the home discounts in upper-income neighborhoods and gated communities -- miles from the urban inner cities the program was designed to help, according to the office of HUD's Inspector General.

Chapter Seven:

GOOD NEIGHBOR NEXT DOOR DISCOUNT PROGRAMS

FIRST RESPONDERS AND TEACHERS may be eligible for a special program offering a 50% discount on the list price of HUD Homes. *Good Neighbor Next Door (GNND) Program* is designed for law enforcement officers, teachers, firefighters, and emergency medical technicians.

Officer Next Door, Firefighter Next Door, EMT Next Door and Teacher Next Door programs discount HUD owned, single-family properties by 50% to qualified teachers and public safety officers. These programs are designed to help reduce crime, raise student test scores, and promote better relations between inner-city residents, police officers, and teachers. These homes are located in designated revitalization areas, subject to a three-year owner occupancy requirement.

HUD requires the purchaser to sign a second mortgage and note for the discount amount. No interest or payments are required on this "silent second" note provided the buyer fulfills the three-year occupancy requirement. The number of properties available is limited and the list of available properties changes weekly.

Good Neighbor Next Door buyers in most cases are able to purchase GNND properties with FHA financing and $100 down payment.

Purchase price for GNND buyers is 50% of list price.

Eligible bidders are first responders -- *police officers, teachers, emergency medical technicians* and *firefighters.*

GNND Criteria:

- Buyer must be employed full time.
- Buyer (and spouse) cannot be a person who has owned real estate in the previous 12 months.
- Buyer must have a reasonable expectation of keeping job for a full year following purchase.
- Buyer must live in GNND property as sole residence for three years following purchase. HUD reserves the right to verify occupancy at yearly intervals.

Bidding on GNND Properties

GNND Timelines	
Deadline	**Listing period**
7 days	Lottery for GNND bidders only
Daily bid opening	Open to multiple buyer types
Various	Sometimes GNND properties are included in general owner occupant and investor offerings.

Chapter Eight:
HOW MUCH SHOULD I OFFER?

How Much Should Buyer Offer?

"How low can I bid?" "How much is the property really worth?" "What do people usually bid on HUD houses?" These are the questions asked over and over in every corner of the HUD Home for Sale kingdom. There are four important factors a buyer should weigh in the process of calculating an amount to bid on a HUD Home:

- Ability to Finance
- Appraised Value
- Comparable Value
- Lowest Net HUD Will Accept

Ability to Finance - Use the lesser of two numbers to arrive at a purchase price for the property – the *Qualifying Number* obtained from the lender, or a *Comfort Zone Number*, the maximum amount you should be spending on a monthly basis for debt service.

Appraised Value - HUD orders an appraisal of the property when it takes title. This number is shown on the property description and is used to determine an initial sale price.

Comparable Value – Complete a Comparative Market Analysis (CMA) of the property for the buyer. A CMA is a detailed analysis comparing several similar SOLD properties located in the area of the HUD home settled in recent months. Online valuation tools like Zillow are handy in areas where their data is on target. In fact, many companies are using Zillow estimates for online valuation and information. Still, consumer cyber valuation tools do not offer the reliability of a CMA prepared by a qualified real estate professional. A competent REALTOR® will compare a single detached home with other single detached homes; he will compare a townhome with another townhome. The online valuation engines mix and match styles, genre, and type in a manner that renders them less useful for comparative data studies.

The Lowest Net HUD Will Accept

Sadly, the new HUD Homes program sacrifices the bid statistic transparency of recent years. There used to be a wealth of information on HUD's websites that listed HUD Homes for Sale bidding and results data. This makes the choice of a competent real estate agent more important than ever. A real estate agent who is working in the trenches with HUD Homes can track bids and results and provide salient advice about a bidding strategy in your area.

HUD will pay the selling brokerage a commission up to 3% for the sale of a HUD Home. The commission amount is deducted from the gross sale price to determine the net proceeds to HUD in calculating a winning bid. (Seller assistance up to 3% is also allowed; this reduces the net amount to HUD in like fashion.)

Example One: Mark McBuyer places an offer on a HUD home. His agent will collect the full 3% commission and he is seeking a 3% seller assist to help him with his closing costs. Proceeds to HUD are calculated as follows:

Example One

Gross Sale Price:	$100,000
3% Listing Agent Commission	3,000
3% Selling Agent Commission	3,000
3% Seller Assist	$3,000
Net Proceeds to HUD	**$91,000**

Example Two: Katie O'Hara places an offer on the same HUD home. Her agent has agreed to work for a maximum 3% commission. She has enough funds for her down payment and closing costs and does not need any funds for assistance. Her gross offer for the property is $3,000 less than Mark's offer, $97,000.

Example Two

Gross Sale Price	$97,000
3% Listing Agent Commission	2,910
3% Selling Agent Commission	2,910
Net Proceeds to HUD	**$91,180**

Note that even though Katie's offer for the property is $3,000 LESS than Mark's bid, the real estate commission and seller assist variables reflect a higher number in terms of net proceeds to HUD. This is the number that really counts when HUD bids are reviewed and selected.

The commission that the real estate agent will receive and how that commission is paid is spelled out in a Business Relationship Agreement between the Buyer and the Buyer Agency. Be clear and upfront and clarify your real estate agent's brokerage policy concerning bids for HUD Homes.

Negotiating the Commission with the Real Estate Agent

A Relationship Agreement between a buyer and a real estate brokerage IS NEGOTIABLE. Have a frank discussion about commission and the duties of the real estate agent before signing a buyer broker contract.

The commission is a highly variable factor with enormous impact on the net income to HUD. Some buyer agents work with retainer agreements for their services and those fees do not appear as a debit to HUD. Retainers are often paid upfront in fee-for-service business consultative real estate business models.

Most real estate agents work on a commission basis, and those fees are paid by HUD.

An offer of $100,000 with a 6% commission (50/50 Local Listing Broker and Selling Broker) will return $94,000 to HUD.

Another offer of $100,000 with a 5% commission ($3,000 to Local Listing Broker and $2,000 to Selling Broker) will return $95,000 to HUD.

If these are the only two offers on the table for a property listed at $100,000, the offer with a lower commission will yield the winning bid.

It is important to discuss the commission at an early stage with the buyer. What is your value proposition as an agent?

Sometimes HUD transactions are very simple. Cash buyers with minimal financial concerns, and properties that are in excellent condition offer real estate agents opportunities for low-maintenance transactions. On the other hand, some buyers require complex financing that includes repair costs. Buyers may receive financial help and advice from family members who want to see the property so that they can offer their input. Some properties are in extreme disrepair and it is necessary to get initial contractor estimates without the benefit of utilities. All of these conditions account for a large time investment by the real estate agent and the agent's commission compensation reflects time projection.

Other considerations:

"Are you viewing the property on a weekend or during evening hours?"

"How many times are you returning to see and inspect the property?"

"Are you showing it to family members for their approval?"

"Are you meeting contractors at the property to help them determine the cost of repairs and renovation?"

All of the scenarios outlined above require the real estate agent's presence and attention. Buyers often fail to consider the time their agents spend post-contract on transaction details and service.

Chapter Nine:

COMPLETING THE PURCHASE OFFER

EXECUTING DOCUMENT CAREFULLY and completely is an important step in the bidding process. Prior to submitting a bid online to HUD, a real estate agent must do the following:

- Fill in ALL the blanks on the HUD contract and all of the addenda, and have each page initialed and/or signed as indicated. Use BLUE INK when you sign the contract.
- Provide all disclosures required by the state with regard to agency law and representation.
- Collect certified funds for the earnest money deposit. Personal checks are NOT acceptable. Be aware that when an offer is accepted, the real estate agent must submit the certified funds with the signed paperwork immediately. The agent certifies at the time of submitting of the bid online that he has certified funds in hand. *The date of the certified check must be on or before the date of online bid submission.*

Earnest money deposits must be in hand before placing a bid online. The funds must be certified, cashier's check or money order, payable to both HUD and the buyer. In the event the buyer's bid is not accepted, the check can be returned to the buyer without the need to deposit the monies in an escrow account, waiting for the check to clear, and writing an earnest money refund check.

Personal and business checks are not acceptable under any circumstances.

Certified fund instrument must have a date preceding or coinciding with purchase agreement signature date.

- Earnest money deposit is $500 for properties up to $50,000.
- Earnest money deposit is $1,000 for properties with a sale price greater than $50,000.
- Earnest money deposit is 50% of the sale price for vacant lots.

Original earnest money check (not a copy) must be included with contract package sent to Asset Manager following accepted bid.

Copies of contracts and checklists are available at www.HUDHomeStore.com at the "Addendums" tab of each property detail page.

Failure of a real estate agent to submit a fully correct form may require changes and initials that must be executed immediately by the buyer upon notice. If an Asset Manager adopts a zero tolerance policy with respect to incomplete contracts, and your contract submission is faulty or incomplete, your contract may be discarded in favor of the next highest offer. Diligence and accuracy are critical to insure a smooth transaction.

I've seen very unhappy buyers working with agents who did not pay attention to small details in HUD transactions. After finding the home of one's dreams, becoming qualified for financing, and submitting a winning bid, buyers' hopes are dashed when a sloppy real estate agent messes up a contract package or tells a buyer he can deliver the earnest money check after the bid results are announced.

The best real estate agents are those who follow the rules without exception. They dot their "i's" and cross their "t's" and take their deals to the settlement table. They are worth every penny of the commission they are paid.

Download your own copy of the "Owner Occupant Sales Package" at a property detail page at HUDHomeStore.com. Read the contract and fill one out completely as an exercise before going "live" with a buyer in real time.

Purchase Agreement Endorsements

Each state has a specific set of addenda that must be included with the main contract form. Some of those addenda include:

Electronic Filing Addendum. After a real estate agent submits the bid online he will print a confirmation sheet with a confirmation number. The electronic filing form will contain information that corresponds to the information on the printed form. Check this carefully so that all information relative to purchaser name, social security number, HUD property address, and sale terms match the signed contract. This addendum must be signed by the purchaser and agent or broker and made part of the agreement.

Owner Occupant Addendum declares that the purchaser will occupy the property as primary residence for at least 12 months and that he has not purchased a HUD property in the previous 24 months.

Radon Gas and Mold Notice. HUD discloses that it has not performed tests for the presence of two conditions that may pose adverse health effects – radon gas and mold. Radon gas is an invisible and odorless gaseous radioactive element that is said to be the second leading cause of lung cancer in the U.S.

Mold is a general term for fungus growth that may or may not be visible. HUD recommends that buyers hire professionals to test for best conditions, and discloses that cost to remedy the problems is the sole responsibility of the buyer.

Lead Based Paint Addenda. There are a series of addenda relative to lead paint. HUD contractors in many areas compile comprehensive reports relative to the presence of lead paint in HUD homes. These reports are made available online prior to the sale in many cases; in cases where they are not available prior to the sale, HUD directs that copies of the reports be sent to the purchaser after the sales contract is executed. Buyers have an opportunity to complete independent inspections.

For Your Protection: Get a Home Inspection. This disclosure underscores the importance of having a home inspection to evaluate the physical condition of the property as well as the mechanical systems. The document points out appraisals serve a different purpose than home inspections. Appraisals are performed primarily to estimate the value of a property and to be sure that minimum property standards are met. This form gives the buyer a chance to opt for a home inspection or to waive it.

Notice to Purchaser Addendum. This addendum must be completed and signed when the bid amount exceeds the appraised value published with the property offering.

Home Inspection Policy. In most areas a buyer has 15 days to complete a property inspection from the date the contract is signed by HUD. Inspections are performed during a two-day window when utilities are activated.

Utility Activation Form. The purchaser must sign a written request to activate utilities so that he can proceed with inspections and appraisals. The purchaser is responsible for the costs to activate and deactivate the utilities and re-winterize the property.

Closing Extension Policy. HUD spells out its closing date extension policy and payment schedule. Buyer's signature attests to receipt of this notice as well as agreement to abide by the policy.

Inspection Addendum to Sale Contract. This document provides notice that HUD does not make warranties about the property and that the Buyer has the option to have the property inspected and then proceed with the contract or cancel it if the inspection uncovers major repair issues the Buyer does not want to undertake.

Forfeiture of Earnest Money Policy. HUD spells out its earnest money policy; in most cases this deposit is held in the closing agent's escrow account. Monies cannot be returned to the Buyer without a written release from HUD.

Understanding What 'As Is' Really Is

HUD Homes are sold in "as is" condition.

- HUD makes no warranties, guarantees, or representations about the property, FHA insurable or otherwise.
- Buyers are not permitted to make repairs on the property prior to settlement. (Exception: Field Service Manager or Local Listing Broker may perform repairs to make the property safe, secure, and marketable.)

- HUD strongly encourages buyers to hire independent homes inspectors.
- Buyers do not acquire repair bills or liens against the title of the property.

FIELD TRIP: Collecting Documents

Follow the links at HUDHomeStore.com, HUD's official web site to the home page for HUD Homes in your state. Download the "HUD Owner Occupant Sale Package" to your computer. You can find the documents at any property detail page at the "Addendums" tab.

Print the documents and use them for reference. Remember, you must obtain the buyer's signature on ALL documents before submitting a bid online!

Chapter Ten:

AFTER YOUR OFFER IS ACCEPTED

IT'S MONDAY AFTERNOON. Bids were due last night at midnight and they will be opened today. "I wonder if I should have bid more." "If I don't get that house I'll never see anything else that I like that much!" "I'm just so excited that I can't concentrate on anything else." These are the thoughts that go through a bidder's mind as anticipation mounts. Bid results will be posted early afternoon.

Your HUDHomeStore.com dashboard awaits.

You take a deep breath and click the link. It's a go! Your bid was accepted! Now what?

The countdown to settlement starts as soon as your bid is accepted and signed. Depending upon the efficiency of the contractor working with HUD, the contract can be signed the same day that the bid is accepted up to two weeks following acceptance. A buyer has 45 days to settle the property from the day the contract is signed.

After the bid is signed, HUD mails an executed copy of the agreement to the real estate agent. In many areas, the agent will also receive a fax correspondence confirming bid acceptance and instructions for processing the transaction.

The following is a schedule of events that will pave the way to a successful transaction.

Week One

✓ Buyer makes formal mortgage application and provides complete documentation for the lender to process the loan. Ask the lender for a checklist and deliver everything on the list as quickly as possible for the lender to verify employment, rental history, and other credit references in a timely manner.

✓ Provide the lender with a copy of the agreement of sale that was sent to HUD. When HUD returns an executed agreement of sale, be sure that the lender receives a copy of it immediately.

✓ Order a Systems Check that complies with the lender's requirements. Check with the lender to see if a home inspection report is sufficient documentation for its processing and underwriting needs. In some cases, lenders require an inspection by qualified contractors (i.e. licensed electricians, heating and air conditioning specialists, etc.). Utilities must be turned on for these inspections.

✓ Counsel the buyer to interview and select home inspectors for the range of inspections that he will need. Some inspectors offer packages with a suite of services. Schedule them to conduct their services before 15 days have elapsed from the time that the contract was signed by HUD. In an FHA transaction the cost of the home inspection (up to $200) can be financed in the mortgage. Possible inspections include:

> *General Home Inspection*
> *Radon Inspection*
> *Termite Inspection*
> *Septic Inspection*
> *Well Inspection*
> *Structural Certification*
> *Roof Certification*
> *Lead Paint Testing*

Mold and Air Quality Testing
Municipal Inspection and Code Report

✓ Order title work through a title company or attorney. There is a closing agent under contract to HUD whose name appears on Line 9 of the main body of the agreement of sale. This agent conducts numerous HUD settlements, is generally highly qualified and knows the ins and outs of this business.
✓ For transactions involving rehabilitation financing like the FHA 203(k), this is the time to contact contractors for estimates on repairs.

Week Two

✓ Plan to be present during the home inspections. The real estate agent is REQUIRED to be present to give the inspector access and ensure the property is returned to the same condition as before the inspection.
✓ Call the lender to be sure that the file is complete and be sure they have ordered an appraisal and sent out written verification requests for employment, rental history, and whatever else is needed to process the loan. NOTE: THERE IS NO APPRAISAL NECESSARY FOR FHA FINANCING! HUD has already completed an FHA appraisal and the lender IS REQUIRED to accept this appraisal if it is less than 150 days old. If conventional financing is involved, the appraiser will need to be scheduled to arrive during the two-day window when utilities are activated.

If major problems surface during the home inspection, this is the time to decide whether or not to proceed with the sale or to cancel the contract.

HUD will NOT complete repairs or reduce the price to reflect a credit for repairs. HUD will return the earnest money deposit to buyers in FHA transactions. HUD says it will keep the earnest money deposit in cash and conventional transactions but it is common practice in some areas to return the earnest money deposit in all cases where inspections reveal serious property deficiencies.

Bear in mind that HUD is not bound to return the earnest money deposit in all cases; there is some discretion at the Asset Manager level that often responds in a friendly and cooperative manner to a polite and efficient transaction management style.

Week Three

✓ Check in with the lender and Closing Agent to ascertain everything is moving along smoothly. Signed contracts from HUD should be in everyone's hands by this point. Be sure that the lender receives a signed copy of the purchase agreement.

Week Four

✓ Check progress with the lender and the title company.
✓ This is the time to file a Contract Extension if the lender requires more time to process the loan application. Don't wait past week four; extensions must be filed 10 days prior to the expiration of the contract. The time to get a handle on this is NOW!

Week Five

✓ Check on title and schedule a time for settlement.

Week Six

✓ Schedule a walk-through inspection of the property prior to settlement, preferably the same day as settlement. Bring padlocks to replace any HUD padlocks and ask the real estate agent to remove the HUD padlocks. There may be hundreds of HUD keys in the hands of real estate agents and numerous "unauthorized" users that fit into that padlock on the door. Don't take any chances on the day of settlement.

DO NOT ...

❖ Perform ANY repairs in the home prior to closing!
❖ Give the buyer a key to the HUD house prior to closing!
❖ Allow the buyer to enter the home without your agent present!
❖ Allow the buyer to move into a HUD home prior to closing!
❖ Allow the buyer to store personal belongings in a HUD property prior to closing!

Chapter Eleven:
THE HOUSE IS YOURS!

CONGRATULATIONS! You are in your new home! It's all yours! For your safety, be sure to re-key the lock after closing. Many real estate agents (and others!) have HUD keys and immediate access to HUD properties. Follow through on repair plans, especially if the lender is holding a repair escrow.

This is no longer a HUD house. This is YOUR home. You can move in now. Enjoy your new home; create some wonderful new memories, and let joy and happiness fill every corner of every room ... in your home and in your heart.

ENJOY your new home IN joy!

Chapter Twelve:

CONSUMER OUTREACH 3.0

IMAGINE THAT YOU HAVE five to ten new listings every week (or more!) without cold calling, without calling on FSBOs or Expired Listing owners. Imagine earning a three percent commission on each sale without the need to co-broke your listings and work with agents from other offices. Imagine another office bears the responsibility for MLS entry but you have the right to advertise and sell these properties. Someone else will take care of cleaning out the debris and securing the property.

You have the fun part of the job -- market and sell the listings.

That's the beauty of working the HUD Homes market.

Are your listings still wearing price tags associated with sellers' fantasies and prices associated with yesterday's reality?

How about working with new listings every week that are priced under market value?

Having trouble making appointments with tenants and sellers whose work schedules make it hard to show your listings? HUD Homes are vacant, and you can show them without an appointment!

When you introduce yourself to the public as a *HUD Homes Specialist*, you will want to consider whether or not to use "HUD Homes" as keywords in your advertising.

I use *Government Owned Homes* as the predominant keywords in my own real estate marketing for several reasons:

❖ The words HUD Homes often conjure images of subsidized rental housing. The words create confusion with buyers who hear this term used more frequently in terms of rental housing than in terms of properties for sale. They may "tune out" the message altogether early in the dispatch.

❖ Some buyers are unfamiliar with HUD and they do not recognize that is an acronym for a federal housing agency.

❖ The term Government Owned Homes opens the possibility of working with other government-owned inventory, especially VA Homes from the U.S. Dept. of Veterans Affairs. (There is a separate contract and another sales process involving the sale of VA properties.) Other state and federal and local agencies also offer properties for sale; each agency has a separate set of guidelines regarding the disposition of its real estate.

HUD Homes Advertising Guidelines

HUD registered real estate brokers must follow strict advertising guidelines.

➢ Properties must not be advertised until the property is officially listed for sale on HUDHomeStore.com.

➢ Properties must be advertised at the listing price and contain a reference to HUD.

➢ Advertising must not convey by word or design an impression that the advertising broker is the sole source of property information or that the broker enjoys any type of listing or sales advantage over other brokers.

➢ Brokers must avoid the use of language that describes HUD Homes as distress sales. HUD insists that HUD certified brokers avoid using the dirty "F" word in advertising HUD Homes: *The word "foreclosure" is forbidden in HUD Homes advertising; the words "repo" and "repossession" are also unacceptable.* Better language to use in advertising is "HUD Owned" and "HUD Acquired" or "Government Owned."

➢ All display advertising of HUD Homes must contain an Equal Housing opportunity logo, statement, or slogan.

➢ Ads must contain flood plain notations where applicable, or other warning information as it appears on the HUD listing on HUDHomeStore.com.

➢ Brokers and real estate agents are not permitted to place business cards, flyers, or signs at HUD properties.

➢ All ads must comply with Truth-In-Lending Act provisos. Details about financing are not allowed since this would require COMPLETE disclosure pursuant to the Act. Advertisements must not contain such statements as: maximum mortgage amount, loan term, or finance charges; the terms "no down payment" or "no closing costs"; and interest rate. The following are permissible: down payment statements that include a precise dollar amount, and general statements such as "easy terms available," "low down payment," and/or "HUD-insured financing available."

➢ Brokers must follow Fair Housing Act guidelines that prohibit housing discrimination based on race or color, national origin, religion, gender, familial status, or handicap.

➢ The Equal Housing Opportunity logo, statement, or slogan must be present on ads to the extent that the law requires it. The three options are:

1. _Logotype:_ If other logotypes are used in the same ad, the Equal Housing Opportunity logo should be of a size at least equal to the largest of the other logos. If no other logotypes are used, then the type should be bold display face, which is clearly visible. Alternatively, when no other logotypes are used, three to five percent of an ad may be devoted to the Equal Housing Opportunity statement.

EQUAL HOUSING OPPORTUNITY

2. _Statement:_ (Bold type) **HUD properties are offered for sale to qualified purchasers without regard to the prospective purchaser's race, color, religion, sex, disability, familial status, or national origin.**

3. _Slogan:_ "Equal Housing Opportunity".

False Advertising Is a Punishable Violation

HUD forbids the use of signage, letterhead, websites, telephone messages, business cards, and office literature using logos or verbiage such as:
- Department of Housing and Urban Development
- Federal Housing Administration
- United States Housing Authority
- Public Housing Administration.

HUD also prohibits using the letters:
- HUD
- FHA
- PHA
- USHA

Additionally, real estate agents and brokers (and others) are warned not to use any combination or variation of those words or the letters:
- HUD
- FHA
- PHA
- USHA

... alone or with other words or letters seasonably calculated to convey the false impression that such name or business has some connection with, or authorization from, the Department of Housing and Urban Development, or any agency thereof is false advertising and IS NOT PERMISSIBLE.

Advertising Permission Timed to Property Listing

HUD registered real estate brokers must follow strict advertising guidelines.

Properties must not be advertised [or shown to buyers] until the property is officially listed for sale at HUDHomeStore.com. Properties must be advertised at the listing price and contain a reference to HUD. It is not necessary to reference the listing brokerage in HUD Home sales. HUD extends blanket permission for all certified HUD brokerages to market and advertise HUD properties.

As soon as a HUD property appears on HUDHomeStore.com, the property is available for sale or marketing. A certified HUD agent does not have to wait until the property appears in the multiple listing service if the property appears on HUDHomeStore.com.

HUD Home advertising that is not property specific is allowed at all times. For example, an ad that references HUD Homes in general terms is acceptable.

Advertising Guidelines: No 'Exclusive' HUD Listings

Advertising must not convey by word or design an impression that the advertising broker is the sole source of HUD Homes property information or that the broker enjoys any type of listing or sales advantage over other brokers. This proviso includes advertising by the listing brokerage.

All certified brokerages are on a level playing field vis-a-vis marketing and advertising.

Chapter Thirteen:

PRINT CAMPAIGNS

I CAN ONLY CHUCKLE when I hear real estate pundits chortle about the demise of newspapers. Certainly, ad pages are down and Internet sites like Craigslist are whittling down the number of total classified advertising pages. Smart real estate agents around the country still use newspaper advertising to gain a competitive edge for HUD Home listings.

Real estate newsroom cultures are changing with the advent of blogs and acquisition of major real estate listing sites like ForSaleByOwner.com.

Anyone who thinks that the creative minds at our nation's newspapers are going to sit back and surrender their business to Internet entrepreneurs is in for a rude awakening. Newspapers and magazines are adapting their business to consumer reading needs, publishing their content on iPads and Kindle devices. Smartphones and tablets display the day's news and headlines to a new generation of readers who passes on paper in favor of the Web.

I wrote my first weekly newspaper column when I was 16 years old. My father was the editor-in-chief of *Printing Magazine*. He wrote an editorial in 1970 predicting the turn of the century would see Americans reading their news at computers.

Some people scoffed at that suggestion. It was a bold prediction, especially since his readership was printing management at large and small printing companies, hot metal typesetting shops, and "new age" phototypesetting shops.

He made that prediction before phototypesetting technology let users create a full page on a computer monitor. Harris-Intertype made headlines shortly afterward with the first system that let typesetters compose a full page on a screen. Now we are reading books on phones!

We've come a long way ... and what's new today may be replaced by something extraordinary tomorrow.

Some real estate marketers scoff at print campaigns. I think a print campaign is key to success in the HUD Homes market.

In fact, I think the print campaigns outlined here are sufficient to attract enough leads to keep the best agents busy for months. Don't write off print advertising. Use it wisely.

Newspaper and Magazine Advertising

Weekend newspapers are a great place to advertise **HUD Homes**. Consider two types of newspaper advertising:

Include the property address and list price as well as telephone information and your web address if you offer information about HUD Homes on your web site.

Write a general ad about HUD Homes in your market area, financing incentives that may be in place (i.e. $100 down payment program) or Good Neighbor Next Door.

Homes magazine advertising requires longer lead time to place ads and it is not practical to use property addresses in homes magazines. However, a stock ad with an invitation to call the office or a 24-hour toll-free hotline with a pre-recorded message will bring a bounty of calls, often surpassing other listing call volume exponentially.

Publish a Newsletter

A good real estate newsletter that showcases HUD Homes should feature information about other real estate products and services, including new and existing inventory that is NOT government owned.

When I decided to carve a niche in the HUD Homes market in the early 90s I used a laser focus for my HUD marketing materials in order not to dilute the message. My message was loud and clear: "I know about HUD Homes. I am the expert." I sent weekly mailings about new HUD listings to my regular subscribers as well as neighbors who lived near the new listings. Sometimes I sent as many as 2,000 pieces of bulk mail on Friday afternoons. There was immediate response to every type of advertising I designed around the government homes market; my newsletter featuring HUD Homes grew dramatically each week.

I contacted past clients as well and many of them requested that I place them on my weekly mailing list.

Within a few months I was startled to see several of my past clients put their properties on the market with other REALTORS®. I was disappointed and dismayed especially since I was enjoying success with my own listing sales. I saw one of my past clients at a supermarket and was surprised when he told me that he was disappointed that he had to hire another REALTOR®, but since "you only sold HUD homes now," he said, "I had to find a new real estate agent."

Those words reverberated in my skull for weeks..."I thought you only sold HUD homes..." Indeed, HUD Homes sales represented a growing part of my real estate practice, but I never limited my practice exclusively to HUD Homes sales. My marketing materials communicated HUD Homes expertise SO WELL that it appeared that the government homes market was the sole focus of my attention.

I learned to communicate the benefits of my work with HUD Homes to my clients. I explain to sellers that the HUD Homes market generates a high volume of new buyer leads; most of those buyers purchase resale properties even though the buyers called for information about HUD Homes. I learned to remind new buyers I was a member of the multiple listings service, and able to show them a full complement of properties – HUD Homes, properties listed in the MLS, and properties sold privately by unrepresented sellers (also known as For-Sale-By-Owners or FSBOs).

I recrafted my newsletter to include information about my own listings on the first page. I wrote about special relocation programs, home warranty plans, and mortgage loan options. I started to conduct more open houses at my listings, and I advertised them in my newsletter.

A well-crafted newsletter combines several writing disciplines:

❖ Apply the succinct and precise verbiage *of classified advertising* to individual property descriptions. Include photos where possible. Consider featuring new or existing in-house listings on the front page. Keep your personal listings showcase separate from the HUD listings to avoid confusion about listings that are government owned and listings that are privately owned and available through an exclusive right to sell listing contract.

❖ Clever *display advertising copy* with multiple call-to-action venues offers the reader a chance to request information via phone, e-mail, or fax. A complementary Internet venue can provide additional information and online updates about property availability.

❖   An *advertorial approach* to article writing establishes the author's credibility and expertise. Example: Newsletter feature article titled "ABC Realty Takes The Secret Out Of Buying Government Owned Homes" offers valuable information at the same time it toots your horn.

ad·ver·to·ri·al *n.* [adver (tisement) + (edi) torial] An advertisement promoting the interest or opinions of a corporate sponsor, often presented in such a way as to resemble an editorial.

There are abundant possibilities attached to printed newsletters. They can be reproduced easily on an office copier. They can be distributed by hand, mailed to a subscriber list, mailed to neighborhoods where HUD Homes are listed for sale, posted on bulletin boards, and inserted into other mailings. Agents who subscribe to personalized newsletter services can tailor a HUD Homes piece that can be inserted easily into the preprinted newsletter.

An e-mail newsletter lets you share information about new HUD Homes listings as soon as they come on the market. Simply copy and paste the listing information to your newsletter. An HTML newsletter with active hyperlinks allows readers to click for additional property details and inspection reports. And, like the print newsletter, you can feature your own listings, notices about open houses, and other real estate services, as well as information about your blog and web site, all with active hyperlinks and calls to action. Make sure your e-mail address and telephone number appear prominently on your website, blog, and everywhere you have a Web presence.

You can design your own templates, subscribe to a newsletter service, or download print and e-mail templates at Microsoft you can use with Word or Publisher programs.

6 Tips to Market HUD Homes to Apartment Dwellers

Here are six tips to connect with renters:

Tip 1. *Create or buy* a list of all the addresses in an apartment complex. Renters comprise the first-time homebuyer market. HUD Homes are usually on the lower end of the price range in each market area and particularly suitable for first-time home buyers. Apartment addresses remain the same when the property turns over to a new tenant. Use a second address line to reduce mailing waste. Example:

John and Jane Arizona
or Current Occupant
1234 Harley Circle Apt. 14
Williams, AZ 55555

Tip 2. *Create a 10-week direct mail campaign.* Renters are always a good source of buyers for HUD Homes. Most areas of the country have affordable housing prices and situations where home ownership trumps renting. Create a campaign of 10 home buying tips. Send tips every other week, with a call to action.

Tip 3. *Use postcards.* Shelf life is short, be sure you have an attention-grabbing headline!

Tip 4. *Always include an irresistible offer* like a special report or a discount or a subscription to a newsletter with a list of all the new HUD Homes on the market. Remember, your goal is to generate leads and turn them into paying customers.

Tip 5. *Have a PLAN to follow up* after someone responds to your irresistible offer. If they ask for a copy of a free report about HUD Homes, call them seven days later to see if they read it. What did they think? Establish dialogue and build rapport with a personal conversation. Have a follow-up plan for one year following your first contact with the person.

Tip 6. *Calculate the approximate monthly mortgage payment* for the HUD Home, including principal, interest, taxes, and insurance (PITI). Target a flyer or a newsletter to apartment complexes that charge monthly rents comparable to the PITI of the HUD Home. Include a line in the piece that asks:

"Did you know that you can own your own home for less than you are paying in rent?"

Renters are always intrigued with the prospect of getting a home at a discounted price and the concept of home ownership has mass appeal among renters in all real estate cycles.

Flyers - SIMPLE and Effective

You may decide to center your marketing efforts on a single HUD property. Occasionally a property in the right location will generate an enormous amount of interest. And, while there will only be one successful bidder for the property, and that bidder may not even be yours, opportunity to market a HUD property in a popular neighborhood can be a catalyst to multiple listings and sales.

1.   **Step One: Prepare a flyer** for the HUD property that is as good as the best flyer you prepare for your own listings. Make sure you identify the property as a HUD Home, indicate that it is available for a limited time only, and include text that says, "This property will be available for several days only. Please call me immediately for more information." Easy flyer templates are available online.

2.   **Step Two: Send or deliver the flyer** to neighbors near the HUD property. Post it in neighborhood convenience stores and other business establishments where patrons are allowed to post flyers. Make sure that your cell phone number is on the flyer and have a pen and paper handy because your phone is going to ring right off of the hook!

Questionnaire and Reply Card

A well-designed questionnaire, in print or on the Web, is a handy tool to gather information about a prospect and to gauge the interest level of a buyer or a seller. Used in conjunction with a marketing piece about HUD Homes, a questionnaire can provide enough information to assess the likelihood of a prospect's intention to engage real estate services in a short- or long-term scenario.

TIP: You can create FREE questionnaires and survey forms on Google Docs. Customize your own template at Google Docs, and design it to match your brand.

Additionally, you can add a line to a card stock CMA card: "Check here for weekly newsletter about government homes."

Insert that CMA/questionnaire card in each mailing piece you send.

Use a questionnaire format occasionally to follow-up with your newsletter subscribers. Send a questionnaire out twice a year to subscribers of both print and e-mail editions of your newsletter. Update information about their real estate needs and ask them if they wish to continue to receive the newsletter so you can update you records.

The questionnaire includes this line with a reply date:

"We would be happy to continue sending you our newsletter, but we must ask that you respond by [select a date] to avoid having your name removed from our mailing list."

Prospects who find value in your newsletter will show no reluctance about completing the rest of the questionnaire. Update their information in your contact database and respond with a handwritten "Thank You" note to personalize your connection. Handwritten notes are a nice touch, especially in this Internet Age.

Postcards

Postcards are probably the simplest and most economical way to share information about HUD Homes. The message on the postcard can be a simple list of HUD Homes addresses and list price. Simple as simple can be.

One of the brokers in the Lehigh Valley, PA, has been dealing almost exclusively in HUD Homes and VA homes for more than 30 years. This gentleman made an excellent living selling HUD Homes without carrying a listing inventory and not even bothering to show MLS listed properties.

His lead generation method is exquisitely simple. He collects the names and addresses of prospects and offers to send them a postcard when new listings come on the market. He sends postcards to a large client base of past HUD Homes buyers. People who receive his postcards pass them to neighbors, family, and friends. He has a bountiful referral business.

In terms of technology and high tech, this broker is a veritable dinosaur. He is known as the local HUD king. Young realty Web wizards wielding tablet computers and Blackberries have a long way to go to capture even a fraction of the market this man held for many years. It is strong testimony to the value of a good work ethic, marketing consistency, and maintaining a solid level of dependability over the long term.

Targeted Direct Mail - Work the Neighborhood

Target the area immediately around a HUD Home for your marketing outreach. You can bet that there are a few neighbors waiting anxiously for word that the house is on the market. The first real estate agent to reach them with details about the HUD Home is likely to be the one who will get their business.

In the early days I worked with HUD Homes I would select one or two houses each week and personally deliver flyers or newsletters to neighbors up and down the street from those HUD Homes. Invariably a neighbor who is renting a similar type of property in the same neighborhood will materialize as an excellent prospect for the HUD Home. Other neighbors are likely to have family and friends who have been waiting for the property to come on the market.

Chatting with neighbors about a HUD property offers important dividends. First and foremost, it gives you a chance to establish yourself as a neighborhood professional, with additional expertise in HUD Homes. Second, it is a good way to gather information about a property and this information will be helpful when it is time to show the property to a prospective purchaser.

Neighbors often have the inside scoop about repairs, problems, and historic details about a HUD property that will further enhance your professional standing with buyers who tour the property with you. Consider collecting contact information from neighbors and ask them if they would like to receive additional information about future HUD Homes that come on the market. Add them to your newsletter list.

As you add prospects to your newsletter list you will have a chance to enhance your image with future buyers and sellers with each mailing.

Chapter Fourteen:

INTERNET MARKETING

YOU MAY CHOOSE TO HAVE YOUR WEBMASTER work
with a programming professional if you want to work with
the data feed from the multiple listing service to display HUD
Homes. However, this data tends to be slow about new
properties coming on the market and there is a delay in
reporting "under contract" status; properties unavailable for
sale continue to display as active listings, sometimes for
longer than a week after a bid is accepted, as paperwork is
processed by the Asset Manager.

A better idea for posting HUD properties online is to take
the information from the HUDHomeStore.com, copy the text
and photographs, then paste the information and enter a few
lines of data about the property on your own website or blog.
It doesn't have to be much: property address, number of
bedrooms and baths, list price, and perhaps the listing
category (i.e. Insured, Insured with Escrow, or Uninsured).

If you want to get really serious with your online
presentation, use additional photos you take yourself and post
some virtual tours! You can guarantee a very loyal following
with enhanced HUD listings on your website or blog.

Make HUD listings a seamless part of your Web presence.

Blogs

Blogs are a great place to talk about HUD Homes and many aspects of the HUD Homes process.

Blog Platforms		
Name	**Price**	**Comments**
RealTown Blogs	FREE	Numerous templates, built-in SEO
WordPress	FREE/ PAID HOSTING	Pay for hosting. This is the state-of-the-art platform for online content management.
Blogger	FREE	Blogger is hosted by Google, free, and easy to use. Blogger.com ceased supporting FTP service in 2010.
ActiveRain	FREE	Primarily a peer-to-peer platform serving real estate and allied professionals.
Point2Agent Blogs	INCLUDED WITH PAID PACKAGE	Point2Agent websites have built-in blogs.There are many blog platforms. A list of popular platforms appears at right. Blogs are websites and easy to maintain. Writing style can be very conversational and readers find blogs highly useful and engaging.

The following are examples of blog posts you can create about HUD Homes:

- How to Buy HUD Homes

- Why I Love to Sell HUD Homes

- HUD Homes with $100 Down Payment

- *Blog about specific HUD Homes*

- Build the Cost of Repairs Into Your Mortgage

- Police Officers Get 50% Discount on HUD Homes

- HUD Homes Price Slashed 50% for Teachers

- The HUD Homes Sales Timeline

- HUD Says, 'Get a Home Inspection'

- FHA Financing is Back in Style

- Low Down Payment Financing on HUD Homes

You can incorporate these blog posts into your real estate blog. Think about an editorial plan for your real estate blog and include a post about HUD Homes once a week. This practice will increase your credibility as a HUD Homes agent and it will add search engine optimization for your website. That makes it easier for the search engine spiders to find your website when prospective purchasers are surfing the web looking for information about HUD Homes.

Getting Social Media Right!

There was never a better time to advertise and market HUD Homes. It was never been easier or more fun to sell government owned homes than it is right now!

Use social media avenues to share the HUD Homes story in your local marketplace. Your blog is your center of gravity. Post articles and listings on your blog and share those links across social media.

Keep your focus! Do not get distracted. The single largest reason most real estate agents fail to monetize their social media presence is lack of focus, lack of discipline.

There are hundreds of social media sites. You cannot be everywhere and execute a good plan. You must choose your venues carefully, and work with a plan. In the following pages we will discuss some larger social media platforms. Don't try to use them all. Spreading yourself thin on social media dilutes your presence. In terms of HUD Homes outreach, select a major real estate portal and two general platforms.

Examples:

Trulia (real estate specific) + **Facebook** + **Twitter**

or

Zillow (real estate specific) + **Facebook** + **YouTube**

If social media is already part of your daily routine, analyze the time you spend there and dedicate some time each week to HUD Homes marketing and outreach. Make it part of a plan. Block time on your schedule.

Stick to it. It will work if you work it!

What Makes You Different?

Social media engagement is staggering. Facebook membership alone may reach one billion in 2011. Real estate agents and brokers and consumers find themselves in online crowds.

The ticket to success in online engagement is uniqueness.

Creating a HUD Homes niche in your local community is a good step to make yourself stand out from the crowd.

There are two genres of social media:

- *General social media populations* feature engagement across industry, academia, government, and everything that falls between those categories. Examples of general social media are Facebook, Twitter, MySpace, and YouTube.
- *Real estate social media platforms* offer property search and other discussion platforms. Examples include Trulia, Zillow, and Yahoo!

All of these platforms offer ways to highlight HUD Homes. We will take several of these platforms and discuss ways you can integrate HUD Homes messaging in each of them.

Social Media Outreach - Facebook
The Ultimate Social Network

Facebook is growing in record numbers.

There are three components of Facebook. Understand the difference between them and engage appropriately:

1. *Personal Profile Page* ... Keep it personal. Don't solicit business on your profile page. You can mention your business on occasion, but keep it light.
2. *Facebook Business Page.* You have two options with Facebook Business Pages: (1) Groups and (2) Fan Pages. If you have a Business Page, consider adding links from blog posts and videos you create about HUD Homes. If you want to make HUD Homes an important part of your market, consider devoting a Facebook Business Page exclusively to HUD Homes in your market area.

Place links to properties and/or blog posts several times a week. Check your page daily for engagement. Ask questions? Probe your fans! Seed engagement and chatter about HUD Homes, financing, home inspections. Use links from your own blog! Facebook Business Pages and Groups will drive traffic to your website.

3. *Facebook Advertising*. Use Facebook advertising to sell HUD Homes. Facebook ads are simple to build. You can advertise to drive fans to your Business Page or drive them to a landing page on your website or elsewhere. Make sure the landing page is a "Wow" page with a call to action and offers consumers an easy way to contact you. Set a daily advertising budget and use the pay-per-click option for best results.

Social Media Outreach - Trulia

Trulia has a social media suite of services, including Trulia Voices questions and answers, Trulia Blogs, and a variety of advertising options.

Here are tips to maximize your Trulia presence for HUD Homes:

✓ *Set up a profile page for free*. Mention HUD Homes as a specialty on the profile page.
✓ *Search Trulia Voices questions and answers* for questions about HUD Homes. Answer several questions, even if they are not in your immediate market area. Some questions about HUD Homes will have the same answers everywhere in the country. FHA 203(k) financing, for example, is administered the same from one state to the next.

✓ *Set up e-mail alerts in your market area.* Be the first real estate agent to answer a question when buyers in your market area ask for help finding affordable housing. Mention HUD Homes in answers to questions on Trulia Voices.

✓ *Start a Trulia blog.* Write blog posts about HUD Homes. Use the links in these blog posts in your Trulia question-and-answer engagement. For example, if someone asks who can buy HUD Homes, you can write an abbreviated answer as well as a link to a blog post that contains more complete information and a call to action.

✓ *Advertise.* Trulia Pro is inexpensive spotlight advertising that lets you target up to 20 market areas. Trulia Pro spotlight advertising is very similar to Facebook advertising - Short headline, photo, and brief text entry. Link the ad to a WOW! landing page. Trulia Local advertising lets you target single zip codes. It is a larger ad, taking up more space on the page. You can include more information here, even a gallery of photographs.

Social Media Outreach - Zillow

HUD Homes are Zillowable.

Zillow is famous for its "Zesstimates" of value for homes. The website is very popular with consumers and the "go to" place online for property valuation inquiries.

✓ *Zillow Advice* is a question-and-answer platform similar to Trulia Voices. You can search for questions related to HUD Homes and allied topics - foreclosures, financing REOs, home inspections, etc.

✓ *Zillow Advertising* options let you buy a percentage of page views in selected zip codes. This is similar to the Trulia Local Advertising. Zillow scored a major coup when it signed a deal with Yahoo! real estate. Zillow now powers the real estate search for Yahoo! Real Estate and Zillow ads appear on Yahoo! Real Estate.

Social Media Outreach - Twitter

Use Twitter to listen to your market.

Twitter offers an uncanny ability to eavesdrop on your local marketplace. A simple Twitter search of "HUD Homes" yields results you can view on a Twitter desktop client like Hootsuite or Tweetdeck.

Twitter is a microblogging platform that lets you broadcast messages up to 140 characters.

You can create a real estate channel with information about HUD Homes and you can create a HUD Homes channel for targeted, focused discussion about government owned properties.

Follow the local press on Twitter and send messages they will find interesting. "50% off HUD Homes for Police Officers" is a tantalizing message for press as well as consumers. You can use a desktop client like Hootsuite [available at Hootsuite.com] and prepare messages in a queue with timed delivery during the day and evening. You can prepare and queue 25 messages in 10 minutes and create a Twitter stream that will last all day.

Telephone and Webinar Outreach

The telephone remains one of the most powerful weapons in your marketing arsenal. The telephone bridges the gap between the majority of buyers who use the Internet in their search for houses and the remaining few who have limited access to the Internet or no access at all. Telephonic marketing may strike a grateful chord with buyers who feel disenfranchised in the looming cyber age. And, the telephone remains a convenient device even for the most "connected" Web surfers.

Caution: Do not undertake a telephone outreach campaign without heeding federal and state "Do Not Call" guidelines. Fines and penalties for violating "Do Not Call" regulations are severe - $11,000 for a first offense!

The telephone is used for numerous types of consumer outreach:

1. *One-on-one call.* A personal phone call is the single most powerful type of outreach possible with the telephone.

Application: Call the residents on a street where a HUD home is located. Tell them that the property is available and offer to send them additional information or schedule a showing.

2. *Telephone IVR systems.* Interactive voice response systems let the user broadcast a message to multiple people at one time. The sender can set setting to deliver the message to live persons who answer the phone, or restrict delivery to answering machines. IVR systems can also be used to send SMS text messages.

Application: Send a broadcast message to people who live in the vicinity of the HUD Home.

3. *Webinars.* Telephones are used in conjunction with Web-based presentation platforms commonly known as Webinars.

Application: Present HUD Home Buying seminars online using Internet and/or telephone.

4. *Fax on Demand* technology allows a caller to receive information via facsimile transmission by means of a telephone call.

Application: This is an excellent complement to a Web interface for information about HUD Homes. It is especially useful in meeting the time sensitive nature of the HUD Homes market, where every day counts. A buyer can call a number and press a number that corresponds to the report he wishes: "Press 10 if you would like a list of HUD Homes." The process is simple and requires no manual intervention.

Create a HUD Homes Hotline

HUD Homes HOTLINE text script:

"Call the HUD Hotline for information about government homes that are available this week. 800-HUD-HOME."

This is a standard line you can use on websites, in the newspaper, in homes magazines, and in flyers and letters. Use a local voice-mail number or a toll-free call capture number with a prerecorded message that lists HUD Homes and the list prices, and gives the caller a chance to leave a message with his contact information.

Keep it very simple. Here is a sample script:

"Thank you for calling ABC Realty's HUD Hotline. The properties that are available this week are:
123 Main Street, Toledo, $60,000
456 Broad Street, Canton, $90,000
Some of these properties are available with financing that lets you build the cost of repairs right in the mortgage. Leave your name and number and the best time to reach you. Have a great day!"

Interactive Voice Response (IVR) technology, unified messaging systems, and standard voicemail products can be used to create a HUD Homes Hotline.

That's it. It is as simple as that. The call capture number will leave a record of the caller's telephone number even if the caller does not identify himself. You'll see that even local real estate agents will call your hotline regularly. Think about the power of the testimony: "Even local real estate agents, my competitors, rely on my HUD Hotline for information about HUD Homes for sale."

What better testimony to affirm your role as the HUD Homes expert in your local market?

Call Capture Technology Rises Above 'Do Not Call' Caution

Call capture technology offers distinct advantages over other types of telephone calls to action in the real estate sales process. Call capture offers a 24-Hour Response Hotline that generates five to seven times as many calls as traditional ad campaigns that rely on human operator pickup.

Here's how it works. The buyer sees an ad about a "HUD Homes Hotline."

The buyer calls the ad to hear a recorded message listing the HUD Homes for sale. The buyer has several choices at the end of the recording:

•   He can leave a message with his contact information and he can leave a detailed request for additional information and a call back.

•   The buyer can elect to receive a fax on demand. The system will automatically accomplish the fax delivery without the need for intervention by the agent.

•   The caller has an opportunity to be connected with an agent immediately by pressing a "0". Studies show that callers who have the opportunity to speak with an agent without having to dial another number are twice as likely to do so than callers who are prompted to call another number to reach an agent.

Regardless of the choice he makes, the system makes a note of his telephone number and sends you a notice about the time of the call and the originating number.

Worried about making calls since the "Do Not Call"rules went into effect? Scared about being hit with a whopping $11,000 fine for a misplaced call?

That's not a concern here. Once a buyer has called a 24-hour-response line, you can call the prospect as often as you like for the next 90 days without having to worry about "Do Not Call" compliance woes.

You can receive your leads by fax or Internet immediately after the prospect completes the call. Some call capture systems can be set up to deliver your leads by pager or cell phone or by e-mail, complete with caller's name and phone number and the source of the call.

Host Your Own HUD Homes Webinar – Online Meetings

Chances are good you receive lots of invitations to attend Webinars to learn more about real estate. Sometimes Webinars are free and often there is a charge connected with registration.

Webinar hosts are able to assemble groups of people together online and use combined audio and video to share information with the audience.

Sponsor your own online HUD Homes Webinar. I teach a continuing education class and designed an online class about HUD Home sales that is offered with two Powerpoint presentations you can customize for your own use:

1. "50% Discount on HUD Homes for First Responders and Teachers"
2. "How to Buy a HUD Home"

You can design your own presentations and share them with consumers in your market area.

There are several good Webinar platforms. Pricing corresponds to the number of Webinar attendees.

GoToMeeting and GoToWebinar have two levels of service. GoToWebinar allows the host to record the Webinar. Once you have recorded a Webinar, you can host the video online and post it on your website or blog.

Additional Webinar platforms:
- Webex
- Yugma
- Microsoft LiveMeeting

HUD Homes Conference Call

Conference call technology is used widely for training and meetings. Coaches and other professionals use paid teleconferencing venues to generate income streams and free teleconferencing to generate new leads for their products and professional services. Real estate professionals have been slow to adopt this technology.

Consider conducting a weekly or a monthly half hour teleconference call and invite prospects to hear an "expert" speak and have a chance to ask questions.

You can bill yourself as the expert speaker or you can moderate the call with special guests. Special guests who are lenders or other types of vendors may appreciate the opportunity to "sponsor" the cost of the call.

Consider a service that offers "recorded calls" as an optional service. You can post pre-recorded calls online at websites. Audio posts are known as podcasts. The "shelf life" of these calls is long term, and the recording can be leveraged to reach a much wider audience than the group that enrolled in the original call.

TIP: Prior to conducting a call, enroll in several "free" teleconference classes with successful teleconference leaders so that you can experience a teleconference firsthand and plan your own session wisely.

Have Fun with HUD Homes!

You will not use all the tools and marketing ideas in this book. What type of marketing works best for you? What is the easiest marketing to use? What is the most fun?

Those are the most important questions to ask yourself … what works for one agent is not always the best answer for another agent.

There are many coaches in the real estate industry who come from the ranks of successful agents in the trenches. They perfected systems that worked for them and they sell their systems to other agents. Replicating another agent's success may work in the short term. If it is not fun and it does not inspire and empower you, it will not work in the long term.

The best chance for success in the HUD Homes market is to find the sweet spot that is fun for YOU. When you greet the day with eagerness and anticipation you know you are on the right track. Do not engage in marketing activities you find cumbersome or tedious. Do not engage in marketing activities because you hear a trainer tell you it's the easiest way to make a fortune.

Printing a few flyers of a property from your MLS may seem like an antiquated approach to marketing. It's "Real Estate 101" and it still works! Trainers are not going to grow a huge following with old advice like printing flyers and knocking on door, so don't expect to hear it at Tech Fairs or real estate conferences. Don't worry about that. Just do it if you enjoy it, and have fun with it.

Look for that sweet spot and go for it!

SUPPLEMENTAL GLOSSARY

184: Properties located on Indian or tribal lands and acquired as a result of foreclosure of a loan guaranteed by HUD's Office of Native American Programs (ONAP) under the Section 184. of the Indian Home Loan Guarantee Program. This is a home mortgage specifically designed for American Indian and Alaska Native families, Alaska Villages, Tribes, or Tribally Designated Housing Entities. Section 184 loans can be used, both on and off native lands, for new construction, rehabilitation, purchase of an existing home, or refinance.

312: Properties acquired as a result of foreclosure of a HUD Community Planning and Development's Rehabilitation Mortgage.

Acquisition: The process through which a real property or mortgage note secured by a real property is conveyed to HUD. Properties and mortgage notes are conveyed (acquired) from a number of sources. See Acquisition Types, Section 2.3.

Adverse Occupants: Occupants who are in possession of a HUD owned or Custodial property without the legal right to be there.

Administrative Contracting Office Staff: After contract award, the HUD official authorized to execute and administer contractual documents based on this task order and who is also responsible for the day-to-day administration of this task order and delegating task order administration responsibilities to contracting staff and Government Technical Representatives.

Acquisition: The process through which a real property or mortgage note secured by a real property is conveyed to HUD. Properties and mortgage notes are conveyed (acquired) from a number of sources.

Affiliated Entity: (a) As to Vendor, any Entity (i) controlling, controlled by, or under common control with the Vendor, or (ii) whose Management Officials are an Immediate Family member of a Management Official of the Vendor; or (b) As to Sub Vendor, any Entity (i) controlling, controlled by, or under common control with the Sub Vendor, or (ii) whose Management Officials are an Immediate Family member of a Management Official of the Sub Vendor, including any agent or broker, licensed under a listing broker, used to list HUD-owned properties; or (c) As to any other Entity, any Entity (i) controlling, controlled by, or under common control with the other Entity, or (ii) whose Management Officials are an Immediate Family member of a Management Official of the other Entity.

"As Is" - HUD Homes are sold in their "as-is" condition. HUD does not warrant the condition of its properties and will not pay for the correction of defects or repairs. Since the new owner will be responsible for making needed repairs, HUD strongly urges every potential homebuyer to get a professional inspection prior to submitting an offer to purchase.

Asset Control Area (ACA) Program: A program for the disposition to eligible participants of HUD-owned properties and future HUD acquisitions of properties and/or mortgage loans located within HUD designated revitalization areas.

Asset Manager: A HUD Vendor responsible for the marketing of HUD REO properties.

Back End Ratio: Indicates the percentage of income that goes toward paying all recurring debt payments, including those covered by the first debt-to-income ratio, and other debts such as credit card payments, car loan payments, student loan payments, child support payments, alimony payments, and legal judgments.

Broken Window: A pane of glass that has a visible opening that permits entry or exposure to the elements or which is so badly cracked as to constitute a hazard, e.g. a window with a crack that divides a single pane into two or more pieces.

Buyback: Properties repurchased by HUD to resolve a post sale claim by the purchaser of a HUD Home.

Casualty Damage: Loss or harm to real or personal property that resulted from an accident, negligence and, or willful destruction, attributed to other than a Vendor, its employees or any affiliated Vendors, Sub Vendors or its employees, or an uncontrollable event such as fire, or some act of nature such as windstorm, snowstorm, or hurricane.

CLTV - Combined Loan to Value: A ratio used by lenders to determine the risk of default by prospective homebuyers when more than one loan is used. In general, lenders are willing to lend at CLTV ratios of 80% and above to borrowers with a high credit rating. (The Value of Loan 1) + (The Value of Loan 2) = Total Value of the Property.

Contracting Officer: The HUD official authorized to execute and administer a contract based on this PWS on behalf of HUD and includes any duly appointed successor or authorized representative.

Control: As to any Entity, the power to direct or cause the direction of the management and policies of such Entity, whether through the ownership of voting securities, by contract, or otherwise. The term "Controlled" shall have a correlative meaning.

Conveyance Condition: Properties that are conveyed free of surchargeable damage (see definition of surchargeable damage).

Cracked Window: A pane of glass that is still intact but may have slight imperfections that do not
amount to an opening in the glass or do not constitute a hazard, e.g. a pane of glass that has been damaged but not broken and there is no danger of falling glass or weather damage to the property.

Custodial Property: A borrower owned property that serves as security for a secretary-held mortgage (including a HECM), which HUD, through the vendor, has taken possession of following default and vacancy or abandonment.

Days: Unless otherwise specified in the Request for Quote (RFQ), all references to days means calendar days.

Debt-to-Income Ratio: The percentage of a consumer's monthly gross income that goes toward paying debts.

Deed in Lieu of Foreclosure: Properties conveyed to HUD by a mortgagee following a deed-in-lieu of foreclosure of an FHA insured mortgage. In this case, a the borrower gave the property to the lender without a foreclosure sale and the lender filed a claim for FHA mortgage insurance.

Defective Service: A service or deliverable that does not meet the performance standard specified in the task order for a specific performance requirement.

Deteriorated Paint: Any interior or exterior painted surface that exhibits cracking, scaling, chipping, peeling, or loose paint.

Electronic Data Interchange (EDI): Software application-to-application communication of data in standard format for business transactions, EDI is a set of standards for structuring information that is to be electronically exchanged between and within businesses, organizations.

Electronic Transmission: A message transmitted electronically in a format displayed on equipment, for example, a personal computer monitor or facsimile machine. The electronic media used to deliver electronic messages displayed on a personal computer monitor includes electronic mail or another method acceptable to HUD.

Emergency Contact Sign: A visible sign on the property that provides a toll free, 24-hour telephone number to report emergencies.

Entity: Any individual, corporation, partnership, joint venture, Limited Liability Company, trust, association.

Fannie Mae: al National Mortgage Association (FNMA); a federally-chartered enterprise owned by private stockholders that purchases residential mortgages and converts them into securities for sale to investors; by purchasing mortgages, Fannie Mae supplies funds that lenders may loan to potential homebuyers. Also known as a Government Sponsored Enterprise (GSE).

FHA: The Federal Housing Administration, generally known as "FHA", provides mortgage insurance on loans made by FHA-approved lenders throughout the United States and its territories. FHA insures mortgages on single family and multifamily homes including manufactured homes and hospitals. It is the largest insurer of mortgages in the world, insuring over 34 million properties since its inception in 1934.

FHA 203(b): FHA's single family program which provides mortgage insurance to lenders to protect against the borrower defaulting; 203(b) is used to finance the purchase of new or existing one to four family housing; 203(b) insured loans are known for requiring a low down payment, flexible qualifying guidelines, limited fees, and a limit on maximum loan amount.

FHA 203(k): This FHA mortgage insurance program enables homebuyers to finance both the purchase of a house and the cost of its rehabilitation through a single mortgage loan.

FHA 203(k) Streamline: FHA's Streamlined 203(k) program permits homebuyers to finance up to an additional $35,000 into their mortgage to improve or upgrade their home before move-in. With this new product, homebuyers can quickly and easily tap into cash to pay for property repairs or improvements, such as those identified by a home inspector or FHA appraiser.

FHA Connection: An Internet-based system that provides FHA business partners and Vendors secure interaction with HUD mainframe systems to perform required reporting and research the origination and servicing history of FHA insured loans.

Field Service Manager: A HUD Vendor responsible for property management, maintenance, and preservation services.

Financial Control Manual: A manual that describes HUD-Single Family Housing Program's uniform policies and procedures for processing and approving vendor invoices related to the marketing of HUD's properties. It also describes the minimum documentary evidence required of each type of Payment Request Transmittal.

First Look: HUD Secretary Shaun Donovan announced a new Departmental initiative that gives state and local governments and nonprofit organizations participating in HUD's Neighborhood Stabilization Program (NSP) preference to acquire homes from the Department's inventory of foreclosed properties (with the exception of Asset Control Area/ACA properties), commonly known as "HUD Homes." Details of the FHA First Look Sales Method have been published as a Notice in the Federal Register. (This program is presently being tested in pilot market areas.)

Flood Zone: Area where coverage under the National Flood Insurance Program may be required in order to obtain a loan.

Foreclosed Secondary Help Mortgages (SHMs): Properties acquired as the result of the foreclosure of a mortgage serviced by HUD including assigned and purchase money mortgages.

Freddie Mac: Federal Home Loan Mortgage Corporation (FHLM); a federally chartered corporation that purchases residential mortgages, securitizes them, and sells them to investors; this provides lenders with funds for new homebuyers. Also known as a Government Sponsored Enterprise (GSE).

Front End Ratio: Indicates the percentage of income that goes toward housing costs. For renters it is the rent amount. For homeowners it is PITI (mortgage principal and interest, mortgage insurance premium [when applicable], hazard insurance premium, property taxes, and homeowners' association dues [when applicable]).

Good Neighbor Next Door Program: Under GNND, HUD offers certain single family properties for sale to police officers, teachers, fire fighters, and emergency medical technicians at 50 percent off of the list price.

Government Technical Monitor (GTM): A HUD employee who assists the GTR in a limited area of expertise and who may be delegated some duties of the GTR.

Government Technical Representative (GTR): A HUD employee who acts as the Contracting Officer's representative in all matters concerning the technical aspects of a task order. The GTR is responsible for giving Vendors technical advice and guidance related to the work required by the task order. Moreover, the GTR is the principal judge of a Vendor's performance, including the quality and timeliness of services.

Health and Safety Hazards: Any condition or situation at the property that exposes the government to abnormal risk, that presents a source of danger, which could cause an accident, or poses the threat of injury, harm to the public or property that must be corrected within one (1) day of discovery or notification.

Home Equity Conversion Mortgage (HECM): A specialized mortgage product available only to senior citizens that allows them to receive cash payments from the equity in their home.

HUD: The U.S. Dept. of Housing and Urban Development is a federa agency whose mission is to create strong, sustainable, inclusive communities and quality affordable homes for all. HUD is working to strengthen the housing market to bolster the economy and protect consumers; meet the need for quality affordable rental homes; utilize housing as a platform for improving quality of life; build inclusive and sustainable communities free from discrimination; and transform the way HUD does business.

HUD-Owned Properties: Those properties that HUD owns by reason of payment of an insurance claim or another acquisition method. Unless otherwise indicated the term includes vacant land and occupied-conveyance properties. HUD-owned properties are also referred to as HUD REO or HUD-homes.

HUDClips: A web-based directory of all of HUD's official policies and directives including notices, Mortgagee Letters, Housing Notices, Handbooks, Code of Federal Regulations and US Codes Titles 12 and 24. The Internet address for HUD's Client Information and Policy System (HUDClips) is
http://www.hud.gov/offices/adm/hudclips/index.cfm

HUD-Owned Properties: Those properties that HUD owns by reason of payment of an insurance claim or another acquisition method. Unless otherwise indicated the term includes vacant land and occupied conveyance properties. HUD-owned properties are also referred to as HUD REO or HUD-homes.

IE - Insurable with repair escrow: This property requires repairs estimated to cost no more than $5,000; it is eligible for an FHA-insured loan provided the purchaser's lender sets up a repair escrow at closing.

Immediate Family: As to any person and whether by blood, law, or marriage, (i) his or her spouse or domestic partner, (ii) his or her children, siblings, or parents, or (iii) the spouses or domestic partners of his or her children, siblings, or parents.

IN = Insurable: This property is eligible for an FHA-insured loan in its current condition.

Lead Based Paint: If a property was built before 1978 it may contain lead based paint. A Lead Based Paint Addendum, which is available from lists of HUD homes for sale, must accompany the contract sent in on behalf of the winning bidder.

Legal Settlement: Properties acquired as a result of a lawsuit or for other reasons. Sometimes HUD accommodates another federal agency to dispose of real estate assets not insured by FHA.

Local Listing Broker: Brokerage provides full listing services on HUD Homes.

LTV - Loan to Value: Ratio of the outstanding debt on a property to the market value of that property.

M&M III Contractors: Management and Marketing (M&M) Contractors manage and market single-family properties owned by, or in the custody of the Department. HUD-owned houses are often referred to as HUD Homes. These are homes that had an FHA-insured mortgage, the homeowners defaulted, and the lender foreclosed. The lender then deeded the home to the Secretary of HUD in exchange for an insurance claim payment. M&M III is a new disposition structure for the management and marketing of its REO inventory that will streamline its operations, capitalize on the expertise of its potential vendors, and provide flexibility to meet changing market conditions in the REO industry.

Management Official: As to any Entity, its owner, partner, principal, shareholder, director, officer, employee, agent, representative, or any individual who directs its daily operations.

Minimum Property Requirements (MPR): The minimum level of quality for existing single-family 1-4 unit properties to be considered technically acceptable for insurance under FHA Programs. MPR can be found in HUD Handbook 4905.1 rev-1 and Mortgagee Letter 2005-48.

Minimum Property Standards (MPS): A minimum quality level acceptable to HUD for new construction single-family 1-4 unit properties.

Mortgage Insurance Premium: In most of FHA programs, HUD collects an Up Front Mortgage Insurance Premium (UFMIP) when the mortgage is closed; and an Annual premium, which is collected in monthly installments.

Mortgagee: A FHA approved mortgage loan holder, originator, or mortgage loan servicer. Mortgagee is also referred to as "Lender".

Mortgagee Compliance Manager: The vendor responsible for performing a variety of pre- and post property conveyance services on behalf of HUD.

Mortgagee Neglect: For a mortgage insured on or after January 1, 1977, the failure by a Mortgagee to inspect, or take reasonable action to preserve and protect a property until conveyance to the Secretary securing an FHA insured mortgage, as required by 24 CFR 203.377. Reasonable action includes initiating foreclosure within the required time frame pursuant to 24 CFR 203.355(b).

NAID: Name and Address Identifier. HUD requires real estate brokers register for NAID number before becoming eligible to bid on HUD Homes

Neighborhood Stabilization Project: The Neighborhood Stabilization Program (NSP) was established for the purpose of stabilizing communities that have suffered from foreclosures and abandonment. The agency is achieving its goal through purchase and redevelopment of foreclosed and abandoned homes and residential properties.

Net Offer: An amount used to determine the winning bidder on competitive sales and to calculate the marketing fee for sales under certain sales methods. Net Offer is calculated by subtracting the dollar amounts of the financing and loan closing costs (that being paid by HUD) and brokers sales commission from the bid price. For discount sales, the amount of the sales discount is not subtracted from the bid price when calculating the Net Offer. For $1 Home sales, the Net Offer equals $1.

Non-Surchargeable Damage: Damage to the property that is not the responsibility of the Mortgagee because it was not caused by Mortgagee Neglect, fire, flood, earthquake, hurricane, tornado, or for condominiums, boiler explosions.

Notice of Acquisition: The notice provided to the Vendor that a property has been assigned to them. Generally, notice is conveyed through P260, however in some cases notice is delivered by the GTR.

Occupied-Conveyance: A formal process through which a Mortgagee receives permission to convey an occupied property to HUD. The term may also be used as a noun to refer to a property conveyed in this manner.

Pass Through Expense: An actual, out of pocket expense incurred and paid by the Vendor that is not deemed a Vendor's expense and which is identified by the Government as eligible for reimbursement.

Performance Evaluation: The GTR/GTM's record of the Vendor's performance under the task order.

Performance Requirement: The service level that separates acceptable performance from unacceptable performance of a task.

Performance Requirements Summary (PRS): A listing of the performance requirements under the task order that the Government evaluates on a regular basis. Performance indicators, standards for these requirements, and surveillance methods will be used to determine if the Vendor meets performance standards.

Performance Standard: The Vendor's performance level on any deliverable as required by the Performance Work Statement.

Personal Identification Verification (PIV): A process for personnel identification and verification to gain user approval and access to HUD's computer systems.

Proposed Rule: Proposed changes to the regulations governing HUD policy as published in the Federal Register.

Quality Assurance (QA): Actions by HUD or its designees to ensure that products or services provided by the Vendor are within the acceptable quality level for a given performance requirement.

Quality Control (QC): Actions taken by the Vendor to control the production of supplies and services to ensure that they conform to the performance requirements and standards. Quality control procedures are outlined in the Quality Control Plan (QCP) developed by the Vendor.

Random Sampling: A quality verification selection method wherein each object in a group has an equal chance of being selected.

Ready to Show Condition: Means the property is free of debris, visible insect/rodent infestations and health and safety hazards. All cabinets, refrigerators, freezers, counter tops, and windows must have been wiped clean and the house must be free of bad smells. All floors and carpets must be clean. All repairs required to correct safety hazards and any approved repairs to be done prior to listing the property must be completed in order for the house to be in ready to show condition. The yard must be free of trash and debris. The grass must be cut, bushes trimmed and holes patched, and or properly secured to protect the public. Swimming pools and wells must be properly secured to protect the public.

Real Estate Owned (REO): An industry term used to describe properties acquired through foreclosure of a mortgage note, or deed of trust. Single-family properties owned by HUD may be referred to as HUD REO.

Reconveyance: The process of returning a property to a Mortgagee by recording a deed in Mortgagee's name and seeking reimbursement for claims paid plus expenses.

Repurchase - Properties repurchased by HUD to resolve a post sale claim by the purchaser of a HUD Home.

Revitalization Area: An area that has been designated by HUD as exhibiting some or all of the following characteristics: a high concentration of HUD homes, low income or low homeownership rates or any other criteria HUD designates. HUD homes within revitalization areas are eligible for discounted sales to certain purchasers.

Revitalization Area Locator (RAL): A web-based geo-mapping tool that is HUD's official source for determining whether a property is located in a revitalization area.

Rework: Corrective actions taken, or to be taken by the Vendor at its own expense and at no additional cost to the Government to rectify defects identified.

Secretary-Held Properties: Borrower owned properties that are the security for mortgage loans held and serviced by HUD either through assignment or origination. Vacant or abandoned secretary-held properties will become Custodial Properties.

Secured Properties: A property where all windows, doors and openings are locked, boarded (where authorized), or otherwise secured to prevent unauthorized entrance by person or animal into any portion of the dwelling, including exterior entrances to crawl spaces, and any other structures on the property, e.g. garages and sheds.

Selling Agent: The Selling Agent in a HUD Home transaction is the agent working for the Buyer.

Special Property Inspections (SPIs): Quality assurance inspections of HUD properties performed by HUD contract inspectors.

Sub Vendor: A person or entity that enters into an oral or written contract or agreement with the Vendor to perform services, including a listing broker used by the Vendor to list HUD-owned properties.

Support Services Contractor (SSC): Contractor responsible for the administration and financial support of the HUD REO Portfolio. The SSC is also responsible for performing financial transmittals, reconciliation of closings, and broker registration services on behalf of HUD.

Surchargeable Damage: Damage to the property (1) by fire, flood, earthquake, hurricane, tornado, or, for condominiums, boiler explosion; or (2) for mortgages insured on or after January 1, 1977, damage caused by a Mortgagee's failure, as required by 24 CFR 203.377, to inspect or take reasonable action to preserve and protect vacant or abandoned properties.

Targeted Sampling: Use of risk based factors rather than random sampling to select properties, files or other subjects for quality assurance or quality control review.

Task Order Award Date: The date upon which HUD and the Vendor have both executed a task order based on the PWS.

Task Order Effective Date: The date upon which the Vendor begins to perform work under the PWS as identified in block 3 of form SF-1449.

Transition Period: A period of time following contract award when a new Vendor develops the infrastructure necessary to perform contractual responsibilities and when those contractual responsibilities are transferred from a Former Vendor (see Section 6) to a new Vendor.

Transmittal: Standard form required under HUD's Financial Control Manual that Vendors must use to request payment of expenses associated with mortgagee compliance, management and the marketing of HUD-owned properties.

UFMIP: The Up Front Mortgage Insurance Premium (UFMIP) must be entirely financed into the mortgage (except for any amount less than $1) or paid entirely in cash and all mortgage amounts must be rounded down to a multiple of $1. Any UFMIP amounts paid in cash are added to the total cash settlement requirements.

UI = Uninsured: This property requires repairs estimated to cost more than $5,000; it is not eligible for an FHA-insured loan, unless a Section 203(k) loan can be arranged.

U.S. Dept. of Housing and Urban Development: HUD is a federal agency with whose mission mission is to create strong, sustainable, inclusive communities and quality affordable homes for all. HUD is working to strengthen the housing market to bolster the economy and protect consumers; meet the need for quality affordable rental homes; utilize housing as a platform for improving quality of life; build inclusive and sustainable communities free from discrimination; and transform the way HUD does business.

Utilities: Gas, electricity and water/sewer services.

VA (Department of Veterans Affairs): VA is a federal agency, which guarantees loans made to veterans; similar to mortgage insurance, a loan guarantee protects lenders against loss that may result from a borrower default.

Vendor: The individual, partnership, corporation or other entity, which is the party subject to the terms and conditions of this task order.

Index